PURSUING A DEEPER

FAITH

CHARLES
STANLEY

OLIVER
NELSON

THOMAS NELSON PUBLISHERS®
Nashville

A Division of Thomas Nelson, Inc.
www.ThomasNelson.com

Published in Nashville, Tennessee, by Thomas Nelson, Inc.

Scripture quotations are from THE NEW KING JAMES VERSION. Copyright © 1979, 1980, 1982, Thomas Nelson, Inc., Publishers.

ISBN 0-7852-7290-9

Printed in the United States

02 03 04 05 PHX 10 9 8 7

CONTENTS

Introduction: God's Invitation   v

1. Preparing for Growth   1
2. Are You Growing? (Part 1)   9
3. Are You Growing? (Part 2)   23
4. Requirements for Growth Toward Intimacy with God (Part 1)   35
5. Requirements for Growth Toward Intimacy with God (Part 2)   46
6. Stages of Growth Toward Intimacy (Part 1)   56
7. Stages of Growth Toward Intimacy (Part 2)   68
8. God's Formula for Spiritual Growth (Part 1)   79
9. God's Formula for Spiritual Growth (Part 2)   91
10. Time Apart with the Lord   102

Conclusion: The Lord Desires Your Presence   111

INTRODUCTION

God's Invitation

Our heavenly Father has issued to each of us a very special two-part invitation. The first part of the invitation is to *know* Him. We are invited not only to know *about* our heavenly Father, but to *know Him*, to be in intimate, personal relationship with Him, and to experience His presence in an ongoing, daily way.

The Invitation to Know God

There is a vast difference between knowing *about* God and *knowing* God. To know about God is to have a head-knowledge of God—to believe that He exists and to draw conclusions about His nature. To know about God is to have an understanding of God and the way in which He works, the commandments He has given for living, and the plan He has implemented for our eternal salvation through Jesus Christ, His Son.

To actually *know* God is something quite different. It is to have a heart relationship with God—to experience His presence and to hear His voice speaking in your spirit on a daily basis, guiding you into the right paths and right decisions that He desires for you. It is to have a deep assurance that you are "locked into" a relationship with Him *forever*, a relationship that cannot be severed by anything that you or another person might do. It is to have confidence of God's love and presence with you always.

A person may know a great deal *about* another person—his name, age, height, color of eyes, profession or occupation, church affiliation, some of his historical background, and so forth. But if you only know *about* a person and do not actually know the person, you cannot answer "yes" to the question "Do you *know* this person?"

To know a person is to know what makes him laugh and what brings tears to his eyes. It is to have shared experiences with him. It is to spend time with him and to converse with him personally and privately—both talking and listening as you exchange confidences, opinions, dreams, hopes, and struggles.

Can we ever fully know God? No. God can never be fully fathomed, known, or loved. He is infinite in His power, wisdom, love, and presence—we are finite. The finite can never fully comprehend or understand the infinite. But we *can* know Him better and better. We *can* experience a deeper and deeper relationship with God.

The Invitation to Become Like Jesus

The second part of God's invitation to each of us is an invitation to become more like Jesus Christ day by day.

Many people believe that all the Lord desires for us is that we be born again—that we accept Jesus Christ as our personal Savior and then continue to believe in Him until the day we die and go to heaven. While the Lord most certainly desires this for each of us, He desires this *and so much more!*

Many people are saved, but it's as if they crossed the threshold into salvation and then never took another step after crossing the threshold. Our life in Christ does not end with a salvation experience. That is only the beginning point. Spiritual growth is to be the norm of our lives, every day of our lives.

In our relationship with the Lord, we are invited to grow spiritually so that we are continually becoming more like Christ

Jesus in our character, which in turn is manifested in behavior. Who we *are* as people is continually to be displayed in how we think and respond to life, what we say, and what we do.

We are to bear the identity of the Holy Spirit at work in us—displaying *His* fruit, which is love, joy, peace, patience, kindness, goodness, faithfulness, gentleness, and self-control (see Gal. 5:22–23). We are to respond to needs as Jesus would respond—with power and love and mercy. We are to think what Jesus would think in response to every situation or circumstance we encounter, and to speak what Jesus would say.

Can we ever fully become like Jesus? No, not in this lifetime. But we are invited—yes, called and challenged—to *become* more like Jesus every day. We are to continue to grow into the fullness of His character.

A Lifetime Challenge

Our quest to have an ever-deepening relationship with our heavenly Father, and our growth into the fullness of Christ's character, is a lifetime challenge. We never reach perfection in our spiritual growth. Neither are we to rest on a plateau of spiritual maturity. We must never assume that we know God as well as we can know Him or that we are as spiritually mature as the Lord desires for us to be.

There's always room for greater growth and a deeper relationship with the Lord.

So let me ask you today . . .

Do you have an intimate relationship with your loving heavenly Father?

Are you growing spiritually? Are you becoming more like Jesus Christ in your character and in your behavior?

God desires today that you be able to give a resounding "Yes" to these questions!

More specifically, I invite you to consider these questions:

- *How do you know you are growing in your relationship with Christ Jesus?*

  _____

  _____

- *What do you consider to be an intimate, personal relationship with your heavenly Father? How would you define this relationship to another person?*

  _____

  _____

- *What do you sense the Lord still desires to share with you, reveal to you, or impart to you?*

  _____

  _____

LESSON 1

PREPARING FOR GROWTH

Each of us has a perspective on the world and on life—a way of looking at things, of judging things, of holding things in the memory. We need to recognize that our perspective is something we have learned, and we need to recognize that we may have adopted a wrong understanding about certain things.

I have found in my years of ministry that a wrong perspective is very common when it comes to spiritual growth. A faulty perspective about God can actually be a major stumbling block toward a person desiring to be in intimate relationship with God.

For example, if a person believes God to be a harsh, punitive, angry judge, that person is likely to shy away from having a relationship with God. On the other hand, if a person believes God to be the only true source of unconditional love, tender mercy, and abundant grace, that person is likely to seek an ever-deepening relationship with God.

In like manner, what we have been taught to believe about Jesus is likely to limit or define the degree to which we believe we can become like Jesus in character, and that, in turn, will determine to a certain degree the limits we place on our own spiritual growth.

In this Bible study you will be challenged to reexamine your own perspective, and to do so against the backdrop of God's Word.

The Bible is our authority when it comes to the nature of God and how to have an intimate relationship with Him. It is our authority when it comes to our spiritual growth. Therefore, it is the reference to which we must return continually to compare what it is that we believe and do with what it is that God *desires* for us. Our perspective is wrong any time it doesn't match up with God's eternal truth.

As you work your way through this study guide, I encourage you to make notes in the margins of your Bible. It is far more important that you write God's insights in your Bible, which you are reading regularly, than to write in this book, although places are provided for you to make notes.

Keys to This Study

You will be asked at various points to respond to the material presented by answering one or more of these questions:

1. What new insights have you gained?
2. Have you ever had a similar experience?
3. How do you feel about this?
4. In what way are you feeling challenged to act?

Insights

A spiritual insight occurs when you read a passage of Scripture and the meaning of that passage suddenly becomes clearer or more applicable to you. You may have read, studied, or meditated on a particular verse or passage many times. But then, God reveals a new level of meaning to you. It's as if the meaning of the Scripture hits you right between the eyes and you feel as if you are reading the passage for the first time.

God desires that we experience insights on a regular basis. Ask Him to give you insights every time you read His Word. I believe He'll answer that prayer. Insights are usually very personal, and they often relate to your experiences, either current or past. In this way, God's Word is always timely and applicable to us, even as it is eternal and universal to all people.

Make notes about your insights. This will be helpful to you in three ways. First, you'll be able to review your insights later in the light of still other Scriptures. You'll find connections among passages of Scripture, and over time, your insight will become even fuller and more meaningful to you. Second, you will find your insight more readily recalled and available for you to share with others as opportunities may arise. Third, you'll find that the more intentional you are about looking for and recording insights, the more insights you will seem to experience. Making notes about your insights is a way of being more intentional and focused in your Bible reading—and the more intentional and focused you are, the more you move into the real depths of God's Word.

Periodically in this study, you will be asked to note what specific passages of the Bible say and mean to you. This is your opportunity to record insights.

Experiences

We each come to God's Word with a unique background. What you read is filtered to a degree by your past experiences.

Relating our experiences to God's Word helps us to see God's Word as being applicable to our lives. You no doubt have said from time to time, "I really know that particular verse is true because I've experienced the truth of it in my life." Now, our experiences don't make God's Word true. The Bible is truth, period. But when we see the Word of God as being applicable to our lives, we have a much keener ability to understand that there isn't anything we experience as human beings that isn't addressed by the Bible in one or more ways. The Bible is about people and about God's relationship to people. And the more we understand how God relates to us, the more we understand about how to grow in our relationship with Him.

Second, the more we see the Bible as relating to our personal experiences, the more the Bible confirms, encourages, convicts, challenges, and transforms us. The net result is spiritual growth. It is as we are encouraged, convicted, and challenged—and subsequently make changes in our lives and are more bold in living out the life of Christ on a daily basis—that we mature in Christ.

As you share your experiences in your spiritual journey with others, you will grow spiritually. Even if you are doing this study on your own, I encourage you to talk to others about your faith experiences. Sharing the truth of God's Word and your relationship to Christ with others *is* a key factor in spiritual growth.

Emotional Responses

Just as we each have our own set of life experiences, so we have our own emotional responses. No one emotional response to God's Word is right or more valid than another. You may feel joy or relief at reading a particular passage, while a person next to you may be frightened or perplexed by the same passage.

I challenge you to do two things as you read and study God's Word:

1. Face your emotional responses to the Bible honestly. Learn to recognize and articulate what it is that you are feeling.

2. Be willing to share your emotions with others. It takes courage to become emotionally vulnerable. Choose to have courage!

As is true about our relating of experience to the Bible, our emotions do not make the Bible *true*. Just because a particular passage of the Scriptures does not bring a tear to your eye or a quickening of your heartbeat does not mean that it is any less applicable or important for your life. All Scripture is vital to every person. We must never shy away from those passages that trouble us, but rather, seek to discover why those passages trouble us. We must never get stuck in reading and studying only those passages that interest us or move us deeply. We must explore, know, and take in all of God's Word.

The value in identifying our emotional response to the Bible is this: When we face and explore how we feel about God's Word, we very often find ourselves confronting what it is that we truly believe about God. And how we feel about God is very often directly related to our desire to know God better and our desire to become more like God's Son.

Allow the Scriptures to touch you emotionally. God created you with emotions. He knows that you feel certain ways toward Him, toward others, toward yourself, and toward His Word. What He desires is that you be in touch with your feelings and be willing to explore ways in which your feelings are in alignment or misalignment with the way Jesus would feel about the Father, others, and you!

The value of sharing emotional responses is linked to building a sense of community. We are called by the Lord to be His "body"—to care for one another, relate to one another, and to love one another. One of the most loving things you can ever do for another person is to listen to how that person feels about God and about His Son, Jesus Christ. One of the most generous things a Christian can do is to share with another person the struggles that he has experienced in overcoming bad teaching or a faulty perspective.

As you meet with others to discuss spiritual growth and your relationship with the Lord, stay focused on what the Bible says. Let the Bible speak for itself. Don't get sidetracked by opinions. It is far more beneficial that you share experiences and feelings than to share what you think about a particular passage. Commentaries have their place, but ultimately, the Bible is a spiritual book that reflects the unfathomable riches of God's own Spirit.

At the same time, do not allow your Bible study group to become a feel-good, emotion-laden, group-therapy session.

Stay in the Word. Relate experiences and emotions to the Word, but continually come back to the Word.

Spiritual growth in one's relationship with the Lord is likely to be a very personal or sacred topic to a person. It is very important that you be sensitive to others and not demand that they express more than they are willing to express. It is very important that you not push another person to confess what he may not be ready to confess, share what he may consider too private to share, or admit to others what he may not have admitted to himself.

Challenges

God intends for us to be challenged by His Word—continually. He has a purpose in communicating with us. He wants us always to be growing more and more like His Son, Jesus Christ. He wants us always to be seeking a deeper relationship with Him. Real growth and intimacy with God do not come about by understanding God's Word alone, but by applying it to our lives and relationships.

In like manner, simply knowing that we have developed a wrong perspective about God or about spiritual growth is not enough. We must be willing to change and to develop in the ways that God desires and that are beneficial to us. Spiritual growth and the development of an intimate relationship with God are not automatic. They require a desire to grow and an act of our will to do those things necessary for growth.

As you read and study God's Word, pinpoint and define—as best you can—areas in which you believe God is challenging you, stretching you, or causing you to trust Him in new ways. Ask yourself, What do I believe God has as the next step for me to take? In so doing, you are identifying a challenge.

God desires to get you into His Word so He can get His Word into you, and in turn, you can share His Word with others. You are likely to find new opportunities to discuss the very things you are learning in this study. Some of them may appear suddenly or seem coincidental. Be aware that God is a master of timing! If He is freeing you in an area or causing you to have insights into a particular aspect of your life, you are going to be transformed in some way as you live in that new freedom or respond to those insights. Others are going to see the "new you." Be bold in sharing with them how the Lord is working in your life.

If you don't have someone with whom you can discuss your insights, experiences, emotions, and challenges, find someone. Perhaps you can start a Bible study in your home. Perhaps you can talk to your pastor about organizing Bible study groups in your church. There is much to be learned on your own. There is much more to be learned as you become part of a small group that desires to grow in the Lord and to understand and apply His Word more fully.

Keep the Bible Central

Again, let me underscore the importance of keeping the Bible central to your study. Come to God's Word as if you are coming to a great banquet table on which to feast until the full longing of your spirit for the things of God is satisfied.

If you are doing a personal Bible study, be diligent in keeping your focus on God's Word. Self-analysis or personal recovery is not the goal. Becoming more like Jesus Christ, entering a new depth of relationship with your heavenly Father, and becoming more reliant and sensitive to the work of the Holy Spirit in your life are the goals.

Prayer

Finally, I encourage you to begin and end each Bible study session in prayer. Ask God to give you spiritual ears to hear what He wants you to hear and spiritual eyes to see what He wants you to see. Ask Him to bring to your mind experiences that relate to what you read. Ask Him to give you new insights.

Ask Him to help you identify your feelings. Ask Him to reveal to you what He desires for you to be, say, and do.

As you end a Bible study session, ask the Lord to imprint on your heart what you have learned so that you will never forget it. Ask Him to transform you into the likeness of Jesus Christ and to show you specific ways you can apply what you read to the situations, circumstances, and relationships in your life right now. Ask Him to give you the courage to follow through and *do* what He is calling you to do. Pray for boldness to be faithful to Him always and to give your witness of His love to others freely.

- *What new insights about spiritual growth and intimacy with God do you hope to gain from this study?*

  _____

  _____

- *Have you struggled in the past with feeling a lack of spiritual growth or the presence of the Lord in your life? What did you do? What were the results?*

  _____

  _____

- *What do you believe may be at work "holding you back" from a deeper relationship with the Lord?*

  _____

  _____

- *Are you open to the possibility of experiencing an intimate relationship with God?*

  _____

  _____

- *Do you desire to be stronger in spirit, and more effective in your spiritual witness and walk?*

  _____

  _____

LESSON 2

ARE YOU GROWING? (PART 1)

What evidence do you have in your life today that you are growing spiritually?

Do you have a means of evaluating spiritual growth?

Many people who attend church just "go through the motions." They may even pray and read their Bibles daily, but they have no evidence of growth or of changes in their life that are linked to their spirituality. Fewer still have an understanding about how to recognize signs of spiritual growth. If you find yourself in one of those categories, this lesson is for you.

God's Call to Growth

God's Word challenges us to grow. Spiritual growth is not an option or a "nice idea"—it is a commandment. In 2 Peter 3:17–18 we read,

> Beloved . . . beware lest you also fall from your own steadfastness, being led away with the error of the wicked; but grow in the grace and knowledge of our Lord and Savior Jesus Christ.

Our lives in Christ are to be lives of continual and steady growth.

- *Do you have a desire to grow? How do you feel about your spiritual growth (or lack of spiritual growth)?*

  _____

  _____

- *As you look back over your life in Christ, cite several ways in which you believe you are growing or have grown.*

  _____

  _____

Do We "Grow" into Salvation?

There are some people who respond to the question "Are you born again?" by saying, "No, not yet, but I'm growing into it."

Of one thing we can be certain—we do not *grow* into salvation. A person is either saved or not saved. A person is never "almost" saved or "about to be" saved as a result of anything he does to initiate or achieve salvation.

The fact is, a person who is not born again is spiritually dead in his trespasses—and dead things don't grow. Since the spiritually dead person cannot grow spiritually, he cannot experience genuine intimacy with God, no matter how much "spirituality" he may claim to have or how much "communion" he may profess to have with God.

Now, before a person is saved, a person may grow in his understanding about who Jesus is, about what Jesus did for him on the cross, about his need for salvation, or about how to receive God's forgiveness. But he does not "grow into" salvation. Salvation is experienced by an act of believing that Jesus is the Christ, the Only begotten Son of God, and by personally accepting what Jesus did on the cross—shedding His blood for the remission of our own sins. Those who confess their sinful nature to God, believe in Jesus and in His sacrificial, atoning death, and receive God's forgiveness through Jesus Christ are born again.

Have you received Christ Jesus as your Savior? That question is crucial for you to answer before proceeding any farther into this study. If you have not been born again in your spirit, you cannot grow spiritually into an intimate relationship with God.

> • *Have you experienced a spiritual new birth by believing in Christ Jesus and accepting Him as your Savior?*

_____

_____

In being born again, a person becomes spiritually alive. As Peter wrote, we are "born again, not of corruptible seed but incorruptible, through the word of God" (1 Peter 1:23). Incorruptible seed is eternal and life-giving, life-producing, life-imparting seed. It is seed that does not die, but continues to live and is expected to produce growth and fruit.

One of the marks of all living things in the natural world is growth. A baby is birthed, and if it is healthy and normal physically, that baby begins immediately to receive nourishment and grow. A baby who fails to grow is diagnosed with "failure to thrive"—a situation that can be deadly if it goes untreated. In the spiritual realm, a newborn believer is expected to grow and develop, to change and mature. A failure to thrive will not bring about spiritual death or a loss of one's salvation, but it can produce a spiritual "deadening"—which can result in a great loss of joy and a significant falling short of that person's potential and purpose in Christ Jesus.

Growth toward maturity is to be the norm of the Christian experience. It is the reason God gave the fivefold ministry to the church (Eph. 4:11–15). It is to be the desire of every believer.

What the Word Says	What the Word Says to Me
And He Himself gave some to be apostles, some prophets, some evangelists, and some pastors and teachers, for the equipping of the saints for the work of ministry, for the edifying of the body of Christ, till we all come to the unity of the faith and of the knowledge of the Son of God, to a perfect man, to the measure of the stature of the fullness of Christ; that we should no longer be children, tossed to and fro and carried about with every wind of doctrine, by the trickery of men, in the cunning craftiness of deceitful plotting, but, speaking the truth in love, may grow up in all things into Him who is the head—Christ. (Eph. 4:11–15)	
The righteous shall flourish like a palm tree, He shall grow like a cedar in Lebanon. Those who are planted in the house of the LORD Shall flourish in the courts of our God.	

They shall still bear fruit in old
age;
They shall be fresh and
flourishing,
To declare that the LORD is
upright;
He is a rock, and there is no
unrighteousness in Him.
(Ps. 92:12–15)

Ten Signs of Spiritual Growth

There are ten means by which we can evaluate whether we are growing spiritually. These are "signs" that appear in the lives of those who are maturing in Christ.

Certainly these signs are not to be used in judging or evaluating other people—we are to evaluate ourselves spiritually, not others. Neither should we assume that all ten signs will appear at all times in all who are growing spiritually. These are ten ways of evaluating positive, healthy spiritual growth—of recognizing a pattern that leads to spiritual maturity.

We will deal with four of these signs in this chapter, and six in the following chapter.

Sign 1: A Growing Hunger to Know God

Those who are growing spiritually have a "hunger" for God. They are not content with knowing Him in an objective way as "Creator," "Savior," or "almighty God." Rather, they desire to know Him as Lord—to know what it is that the Lord desires of them and for them, and to know the experience of the Lord's presence in their lives on a daily basis.

Furthermore, they want to know the fullness of God—Father, Son, and Holy Spirit. Their hunger to know God will extend to a hunger to recognize and respond to the presence of the Holy Spirit on a daily basis.

- *Have you experienced a "hunger" for God in your life? Do you continue to feel that hunger to know Him better?*

  _____

  _____

- *How does it feel to be hungry? In what ways do we feel a hungry spirit?*

  _____

  _____

What the Word Says

What the Word Says to Me

As the deer pants for the water brooks,
So pants my soul for You, O God.
My soul thirsts for God, for the living God. (Ps. 42:1–2)

For this reason I bow my knees to the Father of our Lord Jesus Christ . . . that Christ may dwell in your hearts through faith; that you, being rooted and grounded in love, may be able to comprehend with all the saints what is the width and length and depth and height—to know the love of Christ which passes knowledge; that you may be filled with all the fullness of God. (Eph. 3:14, 17–19)

I determined not to know anything among you except Jesus

Christ and Him crucified.
(1 Cor. 2:2)

But what things were gain to
me, these things I have
counted loss for Christ. Yet
indeed I also count all things
loss for the excellence of the
knowledge of Christ Jesus my
Lord, for whom I have suffered
the loss of all things, and count
them as rubbish, that I may
gain Christ and be found in
Him, not having my own righteousness, which is from the
law, but that which is through
faith in Christ, the righteousness which is from God by
faith; that I may know Him
and the power of His resurrection, and the fellowship of His
sufferings, being conformed to
His death, if, by any means, I
may attain to the resurrection
from the dead. (Phil. 3:7–11)

Sign 2: A Desire to Know God's Truth

The spiritually maturing person will have an *increasing* desire
to know the truth of God's Word.

To know the truth of God's Word extends beyond knowing
what the Bible has to say. It goes beyond knowing Bible stories, Bible commandments, or the words of Jesus. To know the
truth means to know the meaning of the Scriptures and to be
able to make application of them to daily circumstances, situations, and relationships.

Now, we must read God's Word to know God's Word and to be able to take in its truth. So many people, including Christians, read certain magazines and newspapers each day more than they read their Bibles. This is not to discount the value of magazines and newspapers, but rather to call attention to the fact that we think about what we read. What we read has the potential to impact our opinions, our emotions, and our behavior. Surely the Bible should be the top priority on a Christian's daily reading agenda—and it is the top priority for those who are seeking to grow spiritually and develop an intimate relationship with God.

The Word of God is the one sure thing we can count on for truth. It is the one thing that lasts forever in its application to the human heart. There is no greater nourishment for the soul—no greater food that promotes spiritual growth.

- *Do you have an increasing desire to know God's truth? Do you find yourself turning increasingly to the Scriptures to discover God's answers to your questions or God's solutions for your problems?*

What the Word Says

I wait for the LORD, my soul waits,
And in His word I do hope.
My soul waits for the Lord
More than those who watch
for the morning—
Yes, more than those who
watch for the morning. (Ps. 130:5–6)

I rise before the dawning of the morning,

What the Word Says to Me

And cry for help;
I hope in Your word.
My eyes are awake through the
night watches,
That I may meditate on Your
word. (Ps. 119:147–48)

I have chosen the way of truth;
Your judgments I have laid
before me.
I cling to Your testimonies;
O LORD, do not put me to
shame!
I will run the course of Your
commandments,
For You shall enlarge my heart.
Teach me, O LORD, the way of
Your statutes,
And I shall keep it to the end.
(Ps. 119:30–33)

Sign 3: A Greater Sensitivity to Sin and Evil

The person who is growing spiritually will have an increasing ability to discern evil and to recognize sin, and an increasing abhorrence for all that is evil and sinful.

One of the names for the Holy Spirit is the Spirit of Truth. It is the Holy Spirit who sharpens our awareness of error and our ability to distinguish right from wrong. The Christian is a person who is called and enabled to develop a heightened discernment regarding what is pleasing to the Lord and what isn't.

Christians are called to be able to judge right from wrong (see 1 Peter 4:17). This does not mean that we are to judge people—rather, actions and words. It is the Holy Spirit who gives us the ability to "test" spiritual matters to see if they are truly of God, including the testing of things that are taught or preached to us, to discern if they are in line with God's Word (see 1 John 4:1–3).

The person who is maturing spiritually and entering into a more intimate relationship with the Lord is a person who will have an increasing desire to shun evil and to remove himself as far as possible from activities and situations that give rise to sin.

- *Looking back over your life, can you cite things that once attracted you, or in which you once participated, that you no longer find attractive or worthy of your time, energy, or money? How has your desire for righteousness developed? Cite specific examples.*

_____

_____

What the Word Says

Beloved, do not believe every spirit, but test the spirits, whether they are of God; because many false prophets have gone out into the world. By this you know the Spirit of God: Every spirit that confesses that Jesus Christ has come in the flesh is of God, and every spirit that does not confess that Jesus Christ has come in the flesh is not of God. (1 John 4:1–3)

Shun profane and idle babblings, for they will increase to more ungodliness. (2 Tim. 2:16)

What the Word Says to Me

If anyone . . . does not consent to wholesome words, even the words of our Lord Jesus Christ, and to the doctrine which accords with godliness, he is proud, knowing nothing, but is obsessed with disputes and arguments over words, from which come envy, strife, reviling, evil suspicions, useless wranglings of men of corrupt minds and destitute of the truth, who suppose that godliness is a means of gain. From such withdraw yourself.
(1 Tim. 6:3–5)

But let none of you suffer as a murderer, a thief, an evildoer, or as a busybody in other people's matters . . . For the time has come for judgment to begin at the house of God.
(1 Peter 4:15, 17)

Sign 4: A Decreasing Desire for the World's System

The Bible teaches very clearly that although we as believers are *in* this world, we are not to be *of* this world. As believers *in* the world, we must abide by natural law and live within the constraints of man-made laws. We must work and relate to others and provide for ourselves within the "systems" of this world. But, we are not *of* this world—we do not have the same desires and lusts that the world exhibits. We do not have the same dreams, goals, or hopes that sinners have. We desire the things of God, not the things that fulfill the "lust of the flesh, the lust of the eyes, and the pride of life" (1 John 2:16).

I once knew a man who enjoyed going shopping with his wife each weekend. They often traveled a hundred miles or more on a Saturday to shop in nearby cities. One day they said to me, "Since we came to Christ and began to grow in Him, we find that we have far less desire to spend our money on those things that are temporary. Instead, we find ourselves talking more and more about supporting those things that bear eternal fruit." This man and his wife were maturing in the Lord!

The more you "grow up" spiritually, the less desire you will have for material things and the greater your desire will be to invest and participate in those things that have the potential to win souls and bear eternal fruit. Jesus taught, "Do not lay up for yourselves treasures on earth, where moth and rust destroy and where thieves break in and steal; but lay up for yourselves treasures in heaven, where neither moth nor rust destroys and where thieves do not break in and steal. For where your treasure is, there your heart will be also" (Matt. 6:19–21).

The person who is growing spiritually is far more concerned with pleasing God than pleasing men. The opinions of others have little effect on the spiritually mature person; he cares increasingly, however, about what is pleasing to God.

• *In what ways does the world seem to have less of a "grip" on you than it once had? How have your spending habits changed through the years—not only your spending of money, but your spending of time? Do you find yourself less concerned about what sinners say about you, and more concerned about what God might say?*

What the Word Says	**What the Word Says to Me**
Do not love the world or the things in the world. If anyone loves the world, the love of the Father is not in him . . . And the world is passing away, and the lust of it; but he who does the will of God abides forever. (1 John 2:15, 17)	--- --- --- --- --- --- --- ---
For what profit is it to a man if he gains the whole world, and loses his own soul? Or what will a man give in exchange for his soul? (Matt. 16:26)	--- --- --- --- ---
Do not be conformed to this world. (Rom. 12:2)	--- ---
Now we have received, not the spirit of the world, but the Spirit who is from God, that we might know the things that have been freely given to us by God. (1 Cor. 2:12)	--- --- --- --- ---
Set your mind on things above, not on things on the earth. (Col. 3:2)	--- --- ---
Whatever you do, do it heartily, as to the Lord and not to men, knowing that from the Lord you will receive the reward of the inheritance; for	--- --- --- --- ---

you serve the Lord Christ.
(Col. 3:23–24)

Grace to you and peace from
God the Father and our Lord
Jesus Christ, who gave Himself
for our sins, that He might
deliver us from this present evil
age, according to the will of
our God and Father. (Gal.
1:3–4)

- *In what ways are you feeling challenged in your spirit?*

- *In what specific ways is the Lord convicting you of a need to grow spiritually?*

LESSON 3

ARE YOU GROWING? (PART 2)

Every Christian is called to submit daily to the indwelling presence of the Holy Spirit, to seek continuously to be conformed to the likeness of Jesus Christ, and to mature in his faith. "Change for the better" is to be the pattern of the Christian life—God is never content with the status quo of our character development, our witness, our reliance upon Him, or the depth of our relationship with Him. He desires for us each to draw near to Him . . . and nearer still . . . so that He might impart to us the fullness of His presence and His blessings.

In the last lesson, we took a look at four signs of spiritual growth. In this lesson we will take a look at six additional means of evaluating our own spiritual growth.

Sign 5: An Increasing Sphere of Love

The person who is growing in Christ will have an ever-increasing ability to love others. As that love increases, it spreads out to an ever-widening circle of people. The maturing Christian can often look back and say, "I never would have thought I could have reached out to that person with Christ's love." As we mature in Christ, our concern with appearances, status, and personal reputation decreases. Our concern with expressing God's love to the sinner and to the person in need increases.

We find that we are able to forgive people we once thought unforgivable—because we have grown in our understanding that apart from the grace of God, we would be in the same unforgiven state.

We find that we are able to give freely to people without attempts at manipulation—because we have grown in our understanding that we are to give freely what has been given to us: God's mercy and long-suffering kindness.

We find that we are able to love without placing conditions on our love. We are able to say, "I love you" without adding "if you" or "when you" or "unless you" statements—because we recognize that God's love for us is unconditional.

Furthermore, the maturing Christian finds that he is more willing to express love to others—to reach out, to touch, to speak, to share, to listen, to be present in times of need. The person who is growing in Christ has an increasing desire to be used by God to shower His love on others.

- *In your walk with Christ, can you cite specific examples of ways in which your ability to love others has increased? Can you cite specific ways in which you are more willing to express love?*

What the Word Says	What the Word Says to Me
Freely you have received, freely give. (Matt. 10:8)	
If someone says, "I love God," and hates his brother, he is a	

liar; for he who does not love
his brother whom he has seen,
how can he love God whom he
has not seen? And this commandment we have from Him:
that he who loves God must
love his brother also. (1 John
4:20–21)

[Jesus said,] "'You shall love
the LORD your God with all
your heart, with all your soul,
and with all your mind.' This is
the first and great commandment. And the second is like it:
'You shall love your neighbor
as yourself.'" (Matt. 22:37–39)

Finally, all of you be of one
mind, having compassion for
one another; love as brothers.
(1 Peter 3:8)

Sign 6: A Quickness to Forgive Others

The spiritually maturing person finds it easier and easier to forgive those who have wronged him, hurt him, or rejected him. He is more sensitive to the need to forgive those who offend, and he is quicker to make apologies, seek to make amends, and to bring quarrels or disputes to a peaceful resolution.

This does not mean that the spiritually mature person compromises with evil. Nor does it mean that the maturing Christian has a greater desire to be yoked with nonbelievers. Far from it! It does mean that the growing Christian has a desire to live in peace with others, not holding grudges or harboring resentment and bitterness.

When we fail to forgive, we remain tied to a person. To forgive is to set another person free from the binding grip of our heart and to entrust that person to God's care, love, and judgment. It is to let go of all desire for revenge or retribution, and to trust God to work in another person's life according to His plan and purposes.

- *Can you look back on your life in Christ and see a greater awareness of your need to forgive others, and a quicker "response time" in your forgiveness when others hurt you?*

_____

_____

What the Word Says

[Jesus said,] "Love your enemies, do good, and lend, hoping for nothing in return; and your reward will be great, and you will be sons of the Most High. For He is kind to the unthankful and evil. Therefore be merciful, just as your Father also is merciful. Judge not, and you shall not be judged. Condemn not, and you shall not be condemned. Forgive, and you will be forgiven." (Luke 6:35–37)

[Jesus said,] "For if you forgive men their trespasses, your heavenly Father will also forgive you. But if you do not forgive men their trespasses,

What the Word Says to Me

_____

_____

_____

_____

_____

_____

_____

_____

_____

_____

_____

_____

_____

_____

_____

_____

neither will your Father forgive
your trespasses." (Matt.
6:14–15)

Sign 7: An Increasing Desire to Obey God

The person who is growing spiritually will have an ever-increasing desire to keep God's commandments and to obey the voice of the Holy Spirit speaking in his spirit—regardless of circumstances or what others around him are doing. The person who is becoming spiritually mature is less and less influenced by the will of others. He has a stronger and stronger desire to know all of God's commandments and to live according to them.

God's commandments for our lives are not limited to the Ten Commandments or to the laws we find in the Old Testament. They are not even limited to the commandments of Jesus that we find throughout the Gospels and especially in the Sermon on the Mount (see Matt. 5–7). They include the commands that the Lord gives to us by His Holy Spirit on a daily basis—commands to "go here," "do this," "say this," and "give that."

The mature Christian is a person who wants to do God's will. His answer is always yes to God's leading. The more a Christian matures, and the more intimate a relationship the person has with the Father, the quicker the person is to hear God's voice and to respond enthusiastically and with full effort to whatever God commands.

> • *In your walk with the Lord, can you look back and cite experiences in which you were quicker to say yes to God than you once would have been? Can you see a trend toward desiring to know and keep all of God's commandments for your life?*

What the Word Says

[Jesus said,] "Whoever hears these sayings of Mine, and does them, I will liken him to a wise man who built his house on the rock: and the rain descended, the floods came, and the winds blew and beat on that house; and it did not fall, for it was founded on the rock. But everyone who hears these sayings of Mine, and does not do them, will be like a foolish man who built his house on the sand: and the rain descended, the floods came, and the winds blew and beat on that house; and it fell. And great was its fall." (Matt. 7:24–27)

Now it shall come to pass, if you diligently obey the voice of the LORD your God, to observe carefully all His command-ments which I command you today, that the LORD your God will set you high above all nations of the earth. And all these blessings shall come upon you and overtake you, because you obey the voice of the LORD your God. (Deut. 28:1–2)

What the Word Says to Me

Sign 8: Ever-Increasing Faith

The person who is growing spiritually is a person who manifests greater and greater faith—an increased capacity to believe God and to trust God to work in increasingly difficult circumstances or situations.

Many Christians believe that faith is static. They read Romans 12:3: "God has dealt to each one a measure of faith," and conclude that the faith we receive inherently from God is a fixed entity. Jesus, however, spoke of varying degrees of faith. At one point, He chastised His disciples for having "little faith" (see Matt. 14:31). In another incident, He said to a Canaanite woman who came seeking the healing of her daughter, "Great is your faith!" (Matt. 15:28).

Faith is to be exercised. Our faith is capable of growing and becoming stronger the more we exercise or use our faith. The more we trust God to meet our needs and to do those things that only God can do in our lives, the more we see God at work in our lives. And the more God does in us and through us, the more evidence we have of God's presence and power—and the more we are willing to trust Him with even more of our lives. Our faith expands the more we trust God and rely upon God to act in His sovereign way, according to His sovereign timing, and always for His sovereign purposes.

If you are not using your faith to trust God for what may seem to you to be the "impossible," then your faith is not growing.

- *In reviewing your experiences as a Christian, can you cite specific ways in which your faith has grown?*

  _____

  _____

- *Are you trusting God in ways you once never thought to trust God? Do you have an increasing feeling of reliance upon the Lord to meet all your needs?*

  _____

  _____

What the Word Says	What the Word Says to Me
We are bound to thank God always for you, brethren, as it is fitting, because your faith grows exceedingly, and the love of every one of you all abounds toward each other, so that we ourselves boast of you among the churches of God for your patience and faith in all your persecutions and tribulations that you endure. (2 Thess. 1:3–4)	....
For in it [the gospel of Christ] the righteousness of God is revealed from faith to faith; as it is written, "The just shall live by faith." (Rom. 1:17; Hab. 2:4)	....
When Jesus saw their faith, He said to the paralytic, "Son, be of good cheer; your sins are forgiven you." (Matt. 9:2)	....

Sign 9: An Increasing Concern for Others

The person who is growing spiritually will have an ever-increasing concern for the welfare of others, and especially for the spiritual condition of others. He or she will have a strong desire to see sinners receive Jesus Christ as their Savior. He will have a desire to see the practical and emotional needs of others met.

The maturing Christian will have an increasingly soft heart—a tender heart that is sensitive to others and quick to respond in whatever ways are appropriate and possible in meeting needs in others.

We should never forget that Jesus wept over Jerusalem, saying, "If you had known, even you, especially in this your day, the things that make for your peace! But now they are hidden from your eyes. For days will come upon you when your enemies will build an embankment around you, surround you and close you in on every side, and level you, and your children within you, to the ground; and they will not leave in you one stone upon another, because you did not know the time of your visitation" (Luke 19:42–44). Jesus wept at the tomb of His friend Lazarus (see John 11:35). We, too, are called to weep with those who weep and to rejoice with those who rejoice (see Rom. 12:15).

• *As you reflect on your life in Christ, can you see an increased sensitivity in yourself toward the needs of others? Do you find that you are less "hard-hearted" than you once may have been?*

_____

_____

What the Word Says	What the Word Says to Me
Rejoice with those who rejoice, and weep with those who weep. (Rom. 12:15)	
Be kindly affectionate to one another with brotherly love, in honor giving preference to one another; not lagging in diligence, fervent in spirit, serving the Lord; rejoicing in hope, patient in tribulation, continuing steadfastly in prayer; distributing to the needs of the	

saints, given to hospitality.
(Rom. 12:10–13)

Brethren, if anyone among you
wanders from the truth, and
someone turns him back, let
him know that he who turns a
sinner from the error of his
way will save a soul from death
and cover a multitude of sins.
(James 5:19–20)

The fruit of the righteous is a
tree of life,
And he who wins souls is wise.
(Prov. 11:30)

Sign 10: Feelings of Love Toward God

The person who is growing spiritually is going to have increased feelings of love toward God.

Many people feel resentment toward God from their early childhood, or perhaps as a result of something that happened to them as a teenager or young adult. They may have accepted the forgiveness of God by believing in Jesus Christ and His atoning death on the cross, but they continue to fear God, mistrust God, or for any number of reasons, desire a degree of "distance" from God.

The person who is maturing in Christ comes to recognize that God is our loving, merciful, tender, patient heavenly Father—and as such, He can be trusted completely to be our provider, counselor, source of all good blessings, and friend. The early misperceptions about God melt away the more a person comes to know God. And the clearer and more accurate a picture we have of God, the more we desire to be in His presence and know Him fully.

Jesus said that He came to show us the Father. He came to

reveal the nature and character of the Father. When we look at Jesus, we see One who is infinitely approachable, ever-ready to meet the needs of those who come to Him with genuineness of heart, and One who loved to the degree of pouring out His life in sacrifice for others. To know Jesus is to love Jesus. To know Jesus is to know the Father. The more we know the Father, the more we love the Father.

- *As you reflect over your Christian walk, can you see an intensifying of your feelings of love toward God?*

  _____

  _____

- *If you do not have great feelings of love for God today, can you identify the feelings that you do have? Do you know why you have those feelings? Are they in line with the life, character, and love of Jesus?*

  _____

  _____

What the Word Says	What the Word Says to Me
[Jesus said,] "He who has seen Me has seen the Father." (John 14:9)	....
The love of God has been poured out in our hearts by the Holy Spirit who was given to us. (Rom. 5:5)	....
Eye has not seen, nor ear heard, Nor have entered into the heart of man The things which God has	....

prepared for those who love
Him. (1 Cor. 2:9)

    Not all of these signs of spiritual growth may be evident in any one person at any given time. In general, however, the great majority of these signs are manifested by those who are maturing in Christ Jesus. Take a look again at the ten means of evaluation for spiritual growth that we have discussed in these last two lessons and check off those that you believe are true for you:

1. A growing hunger to know God
2. A desire to know God's truth
3. A greater sensitivity to sin and evil
4. A decreasing desire for the world's system
5. An increasing sphere of love
6. A quickness to forgive others
7. An increasing desire to obey God
8. Ever-increasing faith
9. An increasing concern for others
10. Feelings of love toward God

    Are you satisfied with your Christian walk? Are you all that you desire to be when you see Jesus face to face? Do you have an intimate relationship with God?

    If not, ask the Lord today to help you develop a hunger to know Him better and to show you how you might grow in your spirit.

• *What new insights do you have into spiritual growth?*

_____

_____

• *In what ways are you feeling challenged to grow spiritually and to seek a more intimate relationship with God?*

_____

_____

REQUIREMENTS FOR GROWTH TOWARD INTIMACY WITH GOD (PART 1)

To a great extent, spiritual growth is a learning process, a learning that is rooted in the spirit of man, not the mind—but nonetheless a learning process that is based upon acquisition of new knowledge and understanding, and the application of that knowledge in the context of our relationships with God and other people.

All of us know from our years in school that certain skills are considered to be "prerequisite" to the acquiring of other skills. For example, a child needs to learn his letters and numbers before he can read, spell, and do simple arithmetic. The same principle applies to spiritual growth.

There are seven things that are vital for growing in your Christian walk. These are the necessary foundational principles—the "essentials"—required of every person, regardless of age, culture, or denomination. We will discuss three of these prerequisites in this lesson and four in the next.

The Command to Grow

Peter said, "Grow in the grace and knowledge of our Lord and Savior Jesus Christ" (2 Peter 3:18). This statement is in the imperative tense—it is a command to us—and therefore, we can conclude that spiritual growth is something that requires our human will. We do not automatically grow. We must choose to grow spiritually. We must pursue these seven requirements for spiritual growth with our full intention and will. Each of these seven essentials for spiritual growth should be approached with the understanding that we can do these things. The real questions are: Do we want to do them? Are we willing to make the effort to do them? Are we willing to make the changes in our lives that are required for spiritual growth?

> • *How do you feel about God's command to grow in the grace and knowledge of our Lord and Savior Jesus Christ?*

_____

_____

Requirement 1: Renewal of the Mind

Any believer who desires to grow spiritually and move toward a more intimate relationship with God must choose to pursue the renewing of his mind.

Whether you like it or not, you have been preprogrammed to think in certain ways from childhood. You have acquired certain belief systems, opinions, ideas, and perspectives based upon what your parents and other adults around you thought, said, and did. Some of the preprogramming you received was very likely in contradiction to the Word of God, even though your parents may have been Christians and you may have been brought up in the church. No parent is perfect and therefore, no childhood is perfect. We all have a degree of "relearning" to do—some of us more than others.

When the Israelites left Egypt, the Lord recognized that His people had been "Egyptianized" in their thinking and their approach toward life. They had lived as slaves in a land filled with false gods. Much of what the Israelites experienced in their forty years of wandering in the wilderness can be regarded as a "reshaping" of the Israelites' minds and hearts so that they might truly become the people of God, capable and desirous of taking authority over Canaan. In the wilderness, they became a people united under a new law (the commandments of God given to Moses) and with new rituals related to their faith.

Just like the Israelites, we who are born again leave an "alien" land of sinfulness and are on a journey toward the fullness of God's promises and blessings in our lives. We must choose not to be shaped by the world's systems and images, but rather, to be shaped by the Word of God. As we read in Romans 12:2, "Do not be conformed to this world, but be transformed by the renewing of your mind, that you may prove what is that good and acceptable and perfect will of God."

- *What new insights do you have into the need for you to renew your mind, and specifically, into the meaning of Romans 12:2?*

_____

_____

Every gardener knows that it isn't enough for a person to pull up the weeds in a garden. New plants must be planted in the soil once occupied by the weed for the garden truly to flourish and be both productive and beautiful. Untended, unplanted soil will only produce more weeds! In like manner, it isn't sufficient for us simply to be born again in our spirit. We must begin to retrain our spirits and our minds to respond to life as God desires for us to respond. This means a great change in various habits, procedures, thought processes, and belief systems. We must "renew" our thinking, our speaking, and our behaving to line up with our salvation.

How do we do this? By filling our minds with the Word of God. We must read the Bible frequently—at least once a day—and sufficiently. We will know we have read the Bible sufficiently when we find ourselves saying about a particular passage, "I see in this something that I now must do or change in my life."

- *In reviewing your Christian life, in what ways can you see that your mind has been renewed?*

  _____

  _____

- *How do you feel about the need to change your way of thinking—your "worldview"?*

  _____

  _____

What the Word Says

As newborn babes, desire the pure milk of the word, that you may grow thereby. (1 Peter 2:2)

For though by this time you ought to be teachers, you need someone to teach you again the first principles of the oracles of God; and you have come to need milk and not solid food. For everyone who partakes only of milk is unskilled in the word of right-

What the Word Says to Me

----

eousness, for he is a babe. But solid food belongs to those who are of full age, that is, those who by reason of use have their senses exercised to discern both good and evil. (Heb. 5:12–14)

Put off, concerning your former conduct, the old man which grows corrupt according to the deceitful lusts, and be renewed in the spirit of your mind, and that you put on the new man which was created according to God, in true righteousness and holiness. (Eph. 4:22–24)

For the word of God is living and powerful, and sharper than any two-edged sword, piercing even to the division of soul and spirit, and of joints and marrow, and is a discerner of the thoughts and intents of the heart. (Heb. 4:12)

Requirement 2: Readiness to Face Failures

Most of us try to sidestep or justify our failures and faults. We like to take the easy way out, saying, "That's just the way I am" or, "That's the way my parents raised me." The fact is, most of us are not "just the way God wants us to be." In order to get from where we are to where God desires for us to be, we have to make changes in our lives. And that means facing our faults and failures, taking responsibility for them, and going to God with them.

Is there an area in your life in which you seem to have experienced repeated failures? Are you aware of certain faults that you have, and seem always to have had? Have you been trying for years to sidestep, outrun, or ignore those failures and faults in hopes that God will forget about them? Let me assure you today . . . God won't forget them. In His desire to see you made strong, God will continue to pursue those areas in your life that are weak. In His desire to see you made whole, He will continue to pursue those faults and failures that fragment you and cause you disharmony, dysfunction, or uneasiness (feelings of not being at ease, rest, or peace). In His desire to draw you closer to Himself, God will continue to move against any obstacle or barrier that stands in the way of His experiencing genuine spiritual intimacy with you.

The first step each of us must take is to admit our failures, flaws, and faults. We must own up to our finiteness and our weaknesses. And, we must assume responsibility for our failures. We must not seek to blame others for what has happened to us, but to confess to God, "I have brought myself to the place where I am today." Even though others may have wounded you, rejected you, or sinned against you—your response to their actions has made you who you are today. If you truly are to grow spiritually, you must own up to your actions and reactions.

• *How do you feel about your own past faults and failures?*

_____

_____

What the Word Says

If we say that we have no sin, we deceive ourselves, and the

What the Word Says to Me

----

truth is not in us. If we confess
our sins, He is faithful and just
to forgive us our sins and to
cleanse us from all unrighteousness. If we say that we
have not sinned, we make Him
a liar, and His word is not in
us. (1 John 1:8–10)

Search me, O God, and know
my heart;
Try me, and know my anxi-
eties;
And see if there is any wicked
way in me,
And lead me in the way everlasting. (Ps. 139:23)

Confess your trespasses to one
another, and pray for one
another, that you may be
healed. (James 5:16)

Requirement 3: Repentance of Sin

To repent is to turn around, to move in the opposite direction, to make a complete "about-face."

Many people believe that we must repent before we can
receive God's forgiveness. That is not what the Bible says. The
Bible calls us to confess our sins—own up to our sinful state,
admit our need of a Savior, acknowledge our sin nature—and
receive God's forgiveness for our sin. Then, enabled and
empowered by the Holy Spirit dwelling within us, we are to
repent—to change from our wicked ways, our evil attitudes,
hurtful words, and wrong behaviors. No person is capable of
true repentance apart from the power of the Holy Spirit

working within. It is our will plus His power that gives us the willpower to make genuine changes in our lives.

The person who desires to grow spiritually must be willing to change and to give up old sinful habits, desires, lusts, thoughts, and associations.

In 1 Peter 2:1 we read this admonition: "Therefore [since this gospel has been preached to you], laying aside all malice, all deceit, hypocrisy, envy, and all evil speaking . . ."

Peter tells the young believers to lay aside or to "put off" these behaviors. The literal Greek word means to "strip away," as one strips away garments that are tattered and filthy. The believers are told to strip away malice—wicked ill will; guile or deceit—deliberate dishonesty; hypocrisy—pretended piety and love; envy—resentful discontent; and all manner of evil speaking, including slander, backbiting, and lying. Each of these behaviors is subject to the human will. The believers are to repent of these behaviors, or in other words, to change their ways!

The New Testament has a number of similar passages in which believers are admonished to put off or stop one type of behavior, and in its place institute a righteous behavior. Always, these admonitions are given with the understanding that we are capable of doing this according to the power of the Holy Spirit working in us. The changes are not automatic, however. We must want to make them and seek daily to make them.

- *How do you feel about changing those things in your life that you know are contrary to God's desire for you?*

_____

_____

- *Can you cite an experience in the past in which the Holy Spirit helped you to repent of a certain attitude or behavior?*

_____

_____

What the Word Says

Therefore we also, since we are
surrounded by so great a cloud
of witnesses, let us lay aside
every weight, and the sin
which so easily ensnares us,
and let us run with endurance
the race that is set before us.
(Heb. 12:1)

Therefore, putting away lying,
"Let each one of you speak
truth with his neighbor," for
we are members of one
another. "Be angry, and do not
sin": do not let the sun go
down on your wrath, nor give
place to the devil. Let him who
stole steal no longer, but rather
let him labor, working with his
hands what is good, that he
may have something to give
him who has need. Let no corrupt word proceed out of your
mouth, but what is good for
necessary edification, that it
may impart grace to the hearers. And do not grieve the
Holy Spirit of God, by whom
you were sealed for the day of
redemption. Let all bitterness,
wrath, anger, clamor, and evil
speaking be put away from
you, with all malice. And be

What the Word Says to Me

----

kind to one another, tender-
hearted, forgiving one another,
even as God in Christ forgave
you. (Eph. 4:25–32)

[Peter said to Simon,] "You
have neither part nor portion
in this matter, for your heart is
not right in the sight of God.
Repent therefore of this your
wickedness, and pray God if
perhaps the thought of your
heart may be forgiven you. For
I see that you are poisoned by
bitterness and bound by iniq-
uity." (Acts 8:21–23)

Thus says the Lord GOD:
"Repent, turn away from your
idols, and turn your faces away
from all your abominations."
(Ezek. 14:6)

One of the things we must never lose sight of as we grow in our relationship with the Lord is that we love and worship a *HOLY* God. God manifests no darkness, no shadow of turning, no tolerance for evil or deceit. For us to approach God, we must be in a state of forgiveness, which is only made possible as we trust Jesus Christ to be our Savior, Redeemer, Mediator, and Lord. Christ is our forgiveness and our righteousness.

The renewal of the mind, a confession of faults and sins, and repentance of sinful attitudes and behaviors are part of our living in a state of righteousness. They are essential to our drawing close to a Holy God.

Can a person who willfully chooses to pursue the world's

systems and who adopts and displays the world's beliefs draw close to God? No. His thinking and believing are in a direction totally opposite that of the Lord.

Can a person who refuses to acknowledge sin and be forgiven of it draw close to God? No. His sin continues to be a barrier to intimacy with the Lord.

Can a person who refuses to repent of those attitudes and behaviors that he knows are sinful draw close to God? No. His rebellion keeps him from intimacy with a Holy God.

Do you desire today to grow spiritually? Then you must actively choose with your will to address your own sinfulness, choose to change your believing and behavior to line up with God's Word, and choose to wash your mind with the Word of God so that you might be cleansed and renewed in your thinking.

- *What new insights do you have into spiritual growth and intimacy with God?*

  _____

  _____

- *In what ways are you feeling challenged in your spirit?*

  _____

  _____

REQUIREMENTS FOR GROWTH TOWARD INTIMACY WITH GOD (PART 2)

Do you truly desire to grow in your relationship with the Lord to the point where you can say, "I have an intensely personal, intimate relationship with almighty God, my heavenly Father"? Is that your heart's desire?

In the last lesson, we covered three prerequisites for spiritual growth. In this lesson we will deal with four additional essentials for a person to grow in Christ. As we discussed in the previous lesson, these are things that God desires for us and which He enables us to do by the power of the Holy Spirit working in us. These are also things that require our will and effort. We must choose to grow spiritually and to draw close to God.

Requirement 4: Receive Godly Counsel

Every Christian, no matter the state of his spiritual maturity, should have a wise Christian friend with whom he can share his struggles, faults, sins, failures, and spiritual desires and hopes. Ideally, this friend will be a more spiritually mature believer who can serve as a mentor in the faith. If you do not have such a person in your life, I strongly encourage you to seek out such a person.

We each must be open to receiving wise counsel, which is counsel couched in love, forgiveness, and confidentiality. We can learn a great deal from our brothers and sisters in Christ. As we listen to their experiences, we learn how God's Word can be and has been applied in a wide variety of situations and circumstances. We also can benefit greatly from their insights into the truth of God's Word and from their advice regarding our unique God-given plan and purpose in life.

None of us are called to be "lone rangers" in the faith. We are called to relate to one another as a *body* of believers that functions as a family. We are to be interdependent on one another in areas including the sharing of wisdom and knowledge.

In order to benefit from and to give wise counsel, we must choose to be transparent in our own lives and be vulnerable emotionally in the presence of others. We must be candid, forthcoming, and truthful in all we say and do.

The person who does not seek out the wise counsel of others is a person who is limited to his own perspective, deductions, reasoning ability, and information. And that, my friend, is a great limitation no matter how brilliant a person may be!

• *In looking back over your Christian walk, how have you benefited from having wise spiritual counselors and mentors in the faith?*

_____

_____

> • *How does it feel to ask for wise counsel from another believer? How does it feel to be asked for such counsel?*

_____

_____

We never outgrow our need for wise counsel, no matter how spiritually mature we may be. Do not limit yourself to one area of counsel. Get God's wisdom in all areas of your life. Some people need wise counsel in how to be better stewards of their resources, others need wise counsel in how to grow in their prayer life, still others need wise counsel regarding marital or family problems. God's wisdom extends to every area of human existence. You can never receive enough wisdom. If believers around you do not seem to be able to give you wise counsel, go to other sources—perhaps to godly men and women in professional fields or to books or tapes produced by strong Christians. Much of the wisdom of the Christian church through the ages is available to you in books, commentaries, Bible teaching tapes, and other media.

And finally, ask God for His wisdom. Ask the Holy Spirit to be your Counselor, your guide into all spiritual truth. Jesus promised His disciples that He would send them the "Spirit of truth who proceeds from the Father, He will testify of Me" (John 15:26). The Holy Spirit is given to us to "convict the world of sin, and of righteousness, and of judgment" (see John 16:8)—in other words, to enable us to discern at all times good from evil, righteousness from unrighteousness.

What the Word Says

If any of you lacks wisdom, let him ask of God, who gives to all liberally and without reproach, and it will be given to him. But let him ask in faith, with no doubting, for he

What the Word Says to Me

----

who doubts is like a wave of
the sea driven and tossed by
the wind. For let not that man
suppose that he will receive
anything from the Lord; he is
a double-minded man, unstable in all his ways. (James
1:5–8)

[Jesus said,] "I still have many
things to say to you, but you
cannot bear them now. However, when He, the Spirit of
truth, has come, He will
guide you into all truth; for
He will not speak on His own
authority, but whatever He
hears He will speak; and He
will tell you things to come.
He will glorify Me, for He
will take of what is Mine and
declare it to you." (John
16:12–14)

[Jesus said,] "And when He
[the Holy Spirit] has come, He
will convict the world of sin,
and of righteousness, and of
judgment: of sin, because they
do not believe in Me; of righteousness, because I go to My
Father and you see Me no
more; of judgment, because
the ruler of this world is
judged." (John 16:8–11)

My beloved brethren, let every
man be swift to hear, slow to
speak, slow to wrath. (James 1:19)

Requirement 5: Service to Others

We do not learn in isolation. Neither do we grow spiritually
in isolation. We learn and grow in relationship to others.

Many people seem to attend church Sunday after Sunday
without any apparent change in their lives. Church is just
something they "do" on Sunday mornings before they go out
to eat. That is not God's desire!

God desires that we attend church so that we might learn
more about the Lord and His commandments, worship the
Lord with others, pray for our needs, and be inspired to continue steadfastly in the faith. We are then to leave the church
each Sunday and seek as many ways as possible to apply what
we have learned and to tell others what we have experienced
and are experiencing in Christ Jesus.

All of us are to be servants to others in the faith. We are to
minister to the needs of others and to love others. To be of service to others and to love others, we first must be in
relationship with others.

It is as we love and serve others that we discover more about
our own spiritual nature and about how to live the Christian life
effectively and meaningfully. It is as we serve others, both believers and nonbelievers, that we learn more about our own
weaknesses and Christ's strengths. The more we learn about
Christ's strengths and His love, the more we grow in appreciation
of the Lord and the greater our desire to draw closer to Him. What
we learn through service is absolutely vital to our spiritual growth.

> • *In reflecting on your own life in Christ, what have you
> learned about the Lord and about your own spiritual nature
> through service to others?*

What the Word Says	What the Word Says to Me
Through love serve one another. For all the law is fulfilled in one word, even in this: "You shall love your neighbor as yourself." (Gal. 5:13–14)	....
Beloved, if God so loved us, we also ought to love one another. (1 John 4:11)	....
As bondservants of Christ, doing the will of God from the heart, with goodwill doing service, as to the Lord, and not to men, knowing that whatever good anyone does, he will receive the same from the Lord. (Eph. 6:6–8)	....

Requirement 6: Active Reflection About God's Work

A number of years ago, I became acquainted with the writings of an English preacher who died in 1917. I read one book that had been compiled by his wife and was greatly blessed by it. Through the years, I purchased all the available books of his teachings. Even today, Oswald Chambers is a great inspiration to me. I cannot begin to count the number of times I have read *My Utmost for His Highest*.

The biographies of great Christians through the ages are worthy of our reading and reflection. Their life stories allow us to experience vicariously what they have suffered, learned, and accomplished by faith.

It is as we learn about and study the ways in which God has worked in the lives of others—not only the people we read about in the Bible but in the course of history—that we gain an understanding about how God will work in our lives. We can also learn a great deal, of course, by hearing and reflecting upon the ways in which God is working in the lives of other Christians today.

As a boy, I spent four very meaningful days with my grandfather. He was a godly man, a preacher, and I learned much of what I know about trusting God from him as he told me stories of his own experiences in trusting God.

Point out godly character traits in others to your children. Give them patterns to follow as they seek to develop godly traits in their own lives. Actively reflect upon what God is doing, and how He is accomplishing His purposes in and through those who trust in Him. You will learn a great deal, but more important, you will be inspired to grow spiritually and to seek a deeper relationship with your heavenly Father.

- *In your experience, who has inspired you the most to pursue a deeper life in Christ?*

_____

_____

What the Word Says	What the Word Says to Me
[Jesus said,] "Which of these three do you think was neighbor to him who fell among the thieves?" And he said, "He who showed mercy on him." Then Jesus said to him, "Go and do likewise." (Luke 10:36–37)	_____ _____ _____ _____ _____ _____ _____
[Jesus said,] "A disciple is not above his teacher, but everyone who is perfectly trained will be like his teacher." (Luke 6:40)	_____ _____ _____ _____

[Jesus said,] "Most assuredly, I say to you, he who believes in Me, the works that I do he will do also; and greater works than these he will do, because I go to My Father." (John 14:12)

Requirement 7: Responding to Trials

The person who desires to grow spiritually must recognize that every trial and test in life is an opportunity for spiritual learning. So many people believe that when something bad happens to them, the devil caused it to happen. In most cases, the devil had nothing to do with it. The bad consequence is the result of a person's failure or another person's persecution. The fact is, God knows about all of the trials and tests we face in life and He has allowed them to come into our lives for a purpose. Trials and tests are our opportunity to learn more about God's methods, purposes, and perfect plan. They are our opportunities to become strengthened in faith and to prove ourselves worthy of an increased sphere of influence or witness.

If you are to grow spiritually, you must choose not to run from trials and tests, nor to deny their existence. Instead, choose to focus on the Lord as you face a trial. Ask the Lord why He has allowed this in your life. Look for the lesson He desires to teach you or the character trait He desires to develop or strengthen. It is in our trials that the Lord reveals to us His great mercy, strength, and power—which are more than sufficient for any need we face.

God has a way of using every test, trial, failure, and setback we experience for our eternal benefit. Look for the ways in which He is desiring to work in you and through you to bear lasting spiritual fruit.

If we run from trials, we will fail to miss the great lessons we can learn from our trials under the tutelage of the Holy Spirit.

> • *In reviewing your Christian walk, can you cite ways in which trials and tests strengthened you spiritually, caused you to grow spiritually, or deepened your relationship with the Lord?*

_____

_____

What the Word Says

In this you greatly rejoice, though now for a little while, if need be, you have been grieved by various trials, that the genuineness of your faith, being much more precious than gold that perishes, though it is tested by fire, may be found to praise, honor, and glory at the revelation of Jesus Christ. (1 Peter 1:6–7)

Beloved, do not think it strange concerning the fiery trial which is to try you, as though some strange thing happened to you; but rejoice to the extent that you partake of Christ's sufferings, that when His glory is revealed, you may also be glad with exceeding joy . . . If anyone suffers as a Christian, let him not be ashamed, but let him glorify God in this matter. (1 Peter 4:12–13, 16)

What the Word Says to Me

He said to me, "My grace is sufficient for you, for My strength is made perfect in weakness." Therefore most gladly I will rather boast in my infirmities, that the power of Christ may rest upon me. Therefore I take pleasure in infirmities, in reproaches, in needs, in persecutions, in distresses, for Christ's sake. For when I am weak, then I am strong. (2 Cor. 12:9–10)

A significant part of learning occurs when a person has a wise teacher, applies what he learns in active doing, avails himself of the opportunity to learn vicariously from both the mistakes and triumphs of others, and sees life lessons rising from his own hardships and trials. This is not only true in learning with the mind, but it is also true in those things we learn with the heart. Choose to learn all you can about why and how God works, and you will learn great lessons about how to grow spiritually and how to develop an intimate relationship with the Lord.

- *What new insights do you have into the process of spiritual growth toward intimacy with God?*

- *In what ways is the Lord challenging you today to grow spiritually and to draw closer to Him?*

LESSON 6

STAGES OF GROWTH TOWARD INTIMACY (PART 1)

As a Christian matures spiritually, there are several stages that the person goes through as he moves toward an intimate, personal relationship with the heavenly Father. These stages are a normal part of the growth process—they are a natural maturation process.

Just as a healthy baby is born physically with all of the *potential* to develop various adult skills and traits, we are each born spiritually with the potential for great spiritual growth, maturity, and an intimate relationship with the Lord. Not all people choose to develop all of the physical, intellectual, or emotional gifts and talents they have been given. In like manner, not all believers choose to develop all the spiritual potential they have been given. We must choose to develop our spiritual lives, just as we must choose to develop our God-given talents and abilities.

There are four things I want to caution you about as you do this lesson:

First, these stages in spiritual growth are not always clear-cut to us. At times, others close to us can see these stages in our lives more clearly than we see them. Ask the Holy Spirit to reveal to you where you are as you study these stages.

Second, these stages are not for comparative purposes. They are solely for you to use in gaining a better understanding of your level of spiritual maturity, as well as a better understanding of what the Lord may presently be doing in your life.

Third, you can get "stuck" in a phase if you are unwilling to move forward in your spiritual growth. No person can put a stop to your spiritual growth except you. God will not, and others cannot. You must choose not to be discouraged or to turn away from the Lord, but rather, you must choose to push forward in your desire to know God and to become all that He desires for you to be spiritually.

- *Have you ever had an experience in which you felt "stuck" spiritually, as if you weren't growing and didn't know why? What did you do? What was the result?*

  _____

  _____

- *Have you ever felt like giving up in your walk with Christ? Have you ever been so discouraged that you felt like turning away from the Lord? What did you do? What was the result?*

  _____

  _____

Fourth, God is the One who is at work continually to move us from stage to stage. We cannot will ourselves into a new stage. These stages are His work, not ours. At the same time, there are certain things we can do in any given stage to prepare ourselves for the coming stages we face.

As we begin this lesson, I encourage you to read closely the passages below.

What the Word Says

Beware lest you also fall from your own steadfastness, being led away with the error of the wicked; but grow in the grace and knowledge of our Lord and Savior Jesus Christ.
(2 Peter 3:17–18)

We should no longer be children, tossed to and fro and carried about with every wind of doctrine, by the trickery of men, in the cunning craftiness of deceitful plotting, but, speaking the truth in love, may grow up in all things into Him who is the head—Christ—from whom the whole body, joined and knit together by what every joint supplies, according to the effective working by which every part does its share, causes growth of the body for the edifying of itself in love. (Eph. 4:14–16)

As you therefore have received Christ Jesus the Lord, so walk

What the Word Says to Me

----

in Him, rooted and built up in
Him and established in the
faith, as you have been taught,
abounding in it with thanksgiving . . . Let no one cheat you of
your reward . . . not holding
fast to the Head, from whom
all the body, nourished and
knit together by joints and lig-
aments, grows with the
increase that is from God.
(Col. 2:6–7, 18–19)

What things were gain to me,
these I have counted loss for
Christ. Yet indeed I also count
all things loss for the excellence of the knowledge of
Christ Jesus my Lord, for
whom I have suffered the loss
of all things, and count them
as rubbish, that I may gain
Christ and be found in Him.
(Phil. 3:7–9)

Seven Stages of Growth

Stage 1: Unbelief

All of us begin in a stage of unbelief. There was a time in the
life of each Christian in which he did not place his trust in
God, had no desire to know or keep God's commandments,
and was dominated and directed by his fleshly, sinful nature.
As John wrote, "If we say that we have no sin, we deceive ourselves" (1 John 1:8).

What the Word Says	What the Word Says to Me
All have sinned and fall short of the glory of God. (Rom. 3:23)	
Behold, I was brought forth in iniquity, And in sin my mother conceived me. (Ps. 51:5)	
O God, You know my foolishness; And my sins are not hidden from You. (Ps. 69:5)	
All we like sheep have gone astray; We have turned, every one, to his own way; And the LORD has laid on Him the iniquity of us all. (Isa. 53:6)	

Stage 2: Salvation

When we are in a stage of unbelief, the Holy Spirit is nonetheless at work in our lives convicting us of our sinful nature and wooing us to Jesus Christ so that we might receive the forgiveness God makes available through the shed blood of His Son. Our spiritual life truly begins when we accept Jesus as our Savior and receive God's forgiveness and His free gift of the Holy Spirit into our lives.

Believing and receiving are active steps on our part. They require an action of our will. We choose to confess to the Father that we are sinners. We choose to believe that what Jesus did on the cross provides the atonement for our sins and reconciles us to God. We choose to accept God's forgiveness and we choose to receive His Holy Spirit.

Most people who experience God's forgiveness—which we call "salvation" or the "born-again experience"—have feelings of joy and peace. They feel "clean" inside. With salvation also comes a desire to know God, to know what the Bible says, and to share with others what God has done in giving them a "new life."

- *How did you feel when you accepted Jesus as your Savior and received God's free gift of salvation and the indwelling presence of the Holy Spirit?*

_____

_____

What the Word Says

"Come now, and let us reason together,"
Says the LORD,
"Though your sins are like scarlet,
They shall be as white as snow;
Though they are red like crimson,
They shall be as wool." (Isa. 1:18)

[The Lord said,] "I, even I, am He who blots out your trans-gressions for My own sake; And I will not remember your sins.
Put Me in remembrance;
Let us contend together;
State your case, that you may be acquitted." (Isa. 43:25–26)

What the Word Says to Me

....

....

....

....

....

....

....

....

....

....

....

....

....

....

Jesus answered, "Most assuredly, I say to you, unless one is born of water and the Spirit, he cannot enter the kingdom of God. That which is born of the flesh is flesh, and that which is born of the Spirit is spirit." (John 3:5–6)

[Jesus said,] "For God so loved the world that He gave His only begotten Son, that whoever believes in Him should not perish but have everlasting life." (John 3:16)

Stage 3: Service

Those who are born again spiritually have an inevitable desire to serve the Lord in some way. Part of this desire is born of thanksgiving for their salvation; part of it is born of love for God; part of it no doubt is born of a desire to share with those we love the great joy, peace, and assurance about eternity that we have experienced.

Most Christians are properly taught that their service bears fruit and eternal reward (although our acts of service do *not* earn our salvation). Every person has a built-in desire to be of use and to have a purposeful existence. For the Christian, this desire finds its expression in loving service to others, including an active witness about Jesus Christ as Savior. This desire to serve is not a "have to" desire, but a "want to" desire.

- *How has the Lord led you into service since you were born again spiritually?*

What the Word Says	**What the Word Says to Me**
For we are His workmanship, created in Christ Jesus for good works, which God prepared beforehand that we should walk in them. (Eph. 2:10)	....
We should serve in the newness of the Spirit and not in the oldness of the letter. (Rom. 7:6)	....
I beseech you therefore, brethren, by the mercies of God, that you present your bodies a living sacrifice, holy, acceptable to God, which is your reasonable service. (Rom. 12:1)	....

Stage 4: Frustrated Inadequacy

As we serve the Lord to the best of our ability, we come to a place in our service where we realize that our motives are not always pure and our efforts are not always adequate. The result is a frustration at our inadequacy. This frustration can turn quickly to discouragement if we do not come quickly to the truth of God's Word: By yourself, you cannot accomplish anything of eternal value; but with God, you can accomplish all things and produce eternal fruit.

Our feelings of frustration are not only experienced as we serve others. We also may experience feelings of frustration that our prayers aren't powerful enough, our motives aren't pure enough, our attitudes aren't right, our words are ineffective, our praise is hollow, our souls are empty. We come face-to-face with the fact that although we are trying as hard as we can, we are not succeeding in the things that matter most to us.

Paul was the first to admit this stage of frustrated inadequacy. He wrote to the Romans,

> I know that in me (that is, in my flesh) nothing good dwells; for to will is present with me, but how to perform what is good I do not find. For the good that I will to do, I do not do; but the evil I will not to do, that I practice . . . O wretched man that I am! Who will deliver me from this body of death? I thank God—through Jesus Christ our Lord! (7:18–19, 24–25)

• *Have you ever felt like Paul?*

_____

_____

The good news to which we must cling when we experience this stage in our spiritual growth is this: In Christ we are adequate. There is no condemnation to those who are in Christ Jesus (see Rom. 8:1). He is our sufficiency, and in Him, we can do all things that He desires for us to accomplish. We must continue to live and move and have our being in Him.

• *Have you experienced a stage of frustrated inadequacy in your walk with the Lord?*

_____

_____

What the Word Says

I can do all things through
Christ who strengthens me.
(Phil. 4:13)

There is therefore now no con-

What the Word Says to Me

....

....

....

....

demnation to those who are in
Christ Jesus, who do not walk
according to the flesh, but
according to the Spirit. (Rom.
8:1)

And God is able to make all
grace abound toward you, that
you, always having all sufficiency in all things, may have
an abundance for every good
work. (2 Cor. 9:8)

Stage 5: Spiritual Dependency

If we will press forward in our faith and continue to trust
God even though we feel frustrated and inadequate, the
Lord will bring us to a place where we can relax in total
"spiritual dependency" upon Him. When we reach the end
of our own ability and effort, we find that God is able to
work in us and through us in ways we never thought imag-
inable. We find that as we become totally dependent upon
the Holy Spirit for daily guidance, direction, and encouragement, our spiritual walk is more enjoyable and our work
is more effective.

At this stage of our growth, we are actively choosing to
be filled with the Holy Spirit on a daily basis. Now, the
Holy Spirit indwells us at the point of our salvation, but a
daily awareness of His presence and a "filling up" of His
presence to cover our own recognized lack and inability is
something we must request of the Lord and receive from
Him. It is an act of our will. The daily prayer for each of us
must be, "Fill me, Lord, with Your presence. Use me. Work
through me. May my will be totally and completely submitted to Your will so that Your will is done on this earth
today, through me."

• *Have you reached the stage in your life where you have submitted all of your life to Christ and are totally dependent upon Him?*

_____

_____

What the Word Says	What the Word Says to Me
Not that we are sufficient of ourselves to think of anything as being from ourselves, but our sufficiency is from God, who also made us sufficient as ministers of the new covenant. (2 Cor. 3:5–6)	
In Him we live and move and have our being. (Acts 17:28)	
And when they had prayed, the place where they were assembled together was shaken; and they were all filled with the Holy Spirit, and they spoke the word of God with boldness. (Acts 4:31)	

In the next lesson, we will cover the final two stages of spiritual growth toward an intimate relationship with God. Let me ask you at this point:

Do you have a hunger for a deeper walk with the Lord?

Do you have a clearer awareness of where you are spiritually, or where you have been in your spiritual walk?

Are you willing to do what it takes to prepare your heart for the next stage of growth that the Lord has for you?

Press on! Don't give up. The presence and power of God are

worth any struggle, frustration, or restlessness you may ever experience in following Jesus.

- *What new insights do you have into spiritual growth toward intimacy with God?*

  _____

  _____

- *In what specific ways are you feeling challenged in your spirit today?*

  _____

  _____

STAGES OF GROWTH TOWARD INTIMACY (PART 2)

No person is automatically "spiritually mature" at the time he is born again. Just as in natural birth and growth, a new believer must mature in his walk with the Lord. This growth follows a normal pattern and occurs in stages over time. Unlike the physical maturation process, however, there is no accurate predictor of how much time a person may spend in any one stage of spiritual growth. It is the Lord who moves us from stage to stage. Our part is to make the right responses as each stage emerges and develops.

In the last lesson we covered the first five of seven stages toward an intimate, personal relationship with the Lord. In review, these stages are:

1. Unbelief
2. Salvation
3. Service

4. Frustrated Inadequacy
5. Spiritual Dependency

In this lesson we will continue our discussion with the last two stages of spiritual growth.

Stage 6: The "Battle"

A battle erupts in the life of every person who has reached a place of spiritual dependency upon the Holy Spirit. I call this the "Battle of Preprogrammed Bondage." It is a period of increasingly intense restlessness and discontent in one's emotions. The believer knows without doubt that he is dependent upon the Holy Spirit for all effectiveness in ministry and for all joy in living, but at the same time, an inner conflict begins to develop. Questions begin to emerge about one's identity and one's emotional makeup. Many believers find themselves asking for the first time, in all seriousness, "Who am I? Why am I here?" A search for purpose, meaning, and an understanding of one's uniqueness emerges.

- *Have you experienced such a conflict in your life, even knowing that you are born again and filled with the Spirit?*

_____

_____

Many Christians who enter this stage in their spiritual growth believe that the devil is after them—they believe they are under spiritual attack or that the devil is seeking to oppress them or depress them into a return to their old sinful life. While this may be true in a few cases, in the vast majority of cases, it is God who is directly causing this inner restlessness (and in all cases, it is God who is allowing it to occur).

What is God's purpose in this stage? That is the key question we each must ask. The believer at this stage has already dealt with the sin issue of his life, and has come to a place of dependency upon the Holy Spirit . . . but what the believer must now confront is the fact that our sin nature is changed when we are born again, but our emotions and our minds still need to undergo a transformation process.

A person can be born again, serve God, and come through a time of frustration that ends in total dependency upon the Holy Spirit, and still never deal with emotional and mental patterns—attitudes, ways of thinking and rationalizing, feeling, believing, and responding to life—that are carryovers from the "old life." Most of us carry these old patterns with us long into our Christian walk. They are the products of bad teaching, bad example, rejection, hurtful and often abusive experiences, and conditional love. These patterns are like old tapes that play inside us—they manifest themselves in habits, rituals, and behaviors that are not in keeping with God's desire for us. And it is up to us, in this time of God-produced restlessness and discontent, to confront these patterns head-on. God brings us to this point so that we might truly deal with the early lies, deceit, and hurts that we have experienced and that keep us from moving fully into an intimate relationship with Him.

> • *In your life, can you cite several examples of old emotional or attitudinal patterns that in some way cripple you spiritually or that are in conflict with God's truth about your life? Have you experienced bad teaching, bad examples, abuse, hurt, rejection, or conditional love? Have you truly been healed of the wounds inflicted on your heart?*

_____

_____

This "Battle of Preprogrammed Bondage" is a battle that lies entirely within us, although it may manifest itself in bouts of anger (even rage), frustration, depression, and withdrawal from others. The challenge we face is not only to know Christ at this point, but to discover what Christ desires for us to know about ourselves. It is a time for us to confront our past and our inner makeup and to experience God's healing for those areas that lie wounded and scarred deep within.

- *Can you cite examples of the way in which the Lord has healed you of deep inner emotional wounds?*

Why does the Lord wait until we are in this stage of our spiritual life to deal with these things? Probably because to do so earlier would completely devastate us. It seems that a person needs to have a deep assurance of his salvation and his relationship to the Holy Spirit before he can truly trust God to be the healer of his entire being. Any living plant needs to develop roots and reach a healthy size before it is pruned, shaped, or grafted. So, too, with us as believers. Those who have been freed from sin and sealed forever by the Holy Spirit need a time to grow and become established in the Lord before the Lord begins to prune away those things that truly keep us from wholeness.

What we need to keep in mind is that this stage is designed by God for our healing and wholeness as human beings. God desires to restore, replenish, and renew in us things that have been broken, damaged, or stunted.

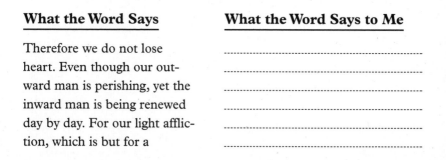

What the Word Says	What the Word Says to Me
Therefore we do not lose heart. Even though our outward man is perishing, yet the inward man is being renewed day by day. For our light affliction, which is but for a	

moment, is working for us a
far more exceeding and eternal
weight of glory, while we do
not look at the things which
are seen, but at the things
which are not seen. (2 Cor.
4:16–18)

Put on the new man who is
renewed in knowledge according to the image of Him who
created him. (Col. 3:10)

The LORD will guide you con-
tinually,
And satisfy your soul in
drought,
And strengthen your bones;
You shall be like a watered gar-
den,
And like a spring of water,
whose waters do not fail . . .
You shall be called the
Repairer of the Breach. (Isa.
58:11–12)

Rejoice in the LORD your God;
For He has given you the for-
mer rain faithfully,
And He will cause the rain to
come down for you—
The former rain,
And the latter rain in the first
month.
The threshing floors shall be
full of wheat,

And the vats shall overflow
with new wine and oil.
So I will restore to you the
years that the swarming locust
has eaten . . .
You shall eat in plenty and be
satisfied,
And praise the name of the
LORD your God,
Who has dealt wondrously
with you;
And My people shall never be
put to shame. (Joel 2:23–26)

The word which came to Jeremiah from the LORD, saying:
"Arise and go down to the potter's house, and there I will
cause you to hear My words."
Then I went down to the potter's house, and there he was,
making something at the
wheel. And the vessel that he
made of clay was marred in the
hand of the potter; so he made
it again into another vessel, as
it seemed good to the potter to
make. Then the word of the
Lord came to me, saying, "O
house of Israel, can I not do
with you as this potter?" says
the LORD. "Look, as the clay is
in the potter's hand, so are you
in My hand." (Jer. 18:1–6)

What should your response be as you face this stage of the "Battle of Preprogrammed Bondage"? I suggest you take these three very positive steps:

First, pray earnestly that the Lord will reveal to you all areas of "bondage" that are limiting you in your emotions and mind. Ask the Lord to reveal those areas where He desires for you to confront your life and make changes or seek healing.

Second, ask the Lord to reveal to you where you might go to receive help or to whom you might go for wise counseling or prayer.

Third, as the Lord reveals various hurts or wounds in your past, burrow into God's Word and seek out the fullness of God's answer of healing to those hurts. And then, receive by your faith the healing that the Lord offers to you. He makes available to you His presence, mercy, forgiveness, and love— He desires that you be whole in spirit, mind, and body.

What the Word Says	What the Word Says to Me
[Jesus said,] "The thief does not come except to steal, and to kill, and to destroy. I have come that they may have life, and that they may have it more abundantly." (John 10:10)	....
Now may the God of peace Himself sanctify you completely; and may your whole spirit, soul, and body be preserved blameless at the coming of our Lord Jesus Christ. (1 Thess. 5:23)	....

There are those who do not have a great deal of bad preprogramming from their childhoods. There are also those who have benefited from good Christian counseling earlier in their Christian walk. These individuals may not experience as intense a battle at this stage of their spiritual growth. Nonetheless, we all face a battle that involves some degree of spiritual error we have taken into our lives.

The work of the Lord in this stage of our spiritual life is, in many ways, an ongoing work. The more the Lord reveals to us about ourselves, the more we recognize that we need His healing presence within us, active at all times, to make us whole. The more we acknowledge that the healing work is His, the more we can relax in His presence and yield to the lessons that He desires to teach us, even those lessons that may be initially painful or uncomfortable.

- *In what ways is the Lord challenging you today to yield to the lessons He desires to teach you about yourself?*

_____

_____

Stage 7: The Exchanged Life

The final stage in our spiritual growth is a stage in which we recognize that the Holy Spirit does not indwell us simply to help us or heal us, but to live Christ's life through us to touch others.

It is in this stage that we truly come not only to believe with our heart but to embody in our whole life the truth that Christ dwells within us and that the life we live is no longer our own, but His. Everything is yielded to Him. We no longer have dreams, goals, or desires that are exclusively our own—rather, our dreams, goals, and desires flow from what He dreams, desires, and has planned on our behalf. The sole purpose of our lives is to know Christ and to be His instrument of righteousness in this world. Our heart's desire is to be used by Him for His eternal purposes.

- *Have you come to the stage where you can say, "It is not I who live, but Christ in me"?*

_____

_____

In this final stage of our spiritual growth, we have a deep hunger for the Lord. We desire to spend more time with Him, to know Him more intimately, and to enter into long periods of prayer and study of the Scriptures so that we might hear His voice more clearly and know His heart more fully. Nothing gives us as much joy as spending time with the Lord. Nothing energizes us as much as hearing a directive or a word of encouragement from the Lord. We live to praise and serve the Lord in all we say and do.

What the Word Says	What the Word Says to Me
Because Your lovingkindness is better than life,	....
My lips shall praise You.	....
Thus I will bless You while I live;	....
I will lift up my hands in Your name.	....
My soul shall be satisfied as with marrow and fatness,	....
And my mouth shall praise You with joyful lips.	....
When I remember You on my bed,	....
I meditate on You in the night watches.	....
Because You have been my help,	....
Therefore in the shadow of	....

Your wings I will rejoice.
My soul follows close behind
You;
Your right hand upholds me.
(Ps. 63:3–8)

I have been crucified with
Christ; it is no longer I who
live, but Christ lives in me; and
the life which I now live in the
flesh I live by faith in the Son
of God, who loved me and gave
Himself for me. (Gal. 2:20)

For me, to live is Christ, and
to die is gain. (Phil. 1:21)

Not that I have already
attained, or am already perfected; but I press on, that I
may lay hold of that for which
Christ Jesus has also laid hold
of me. Brethren, I do not
count myself to have appre-
hended; but one thing I do,
forgetting those things which
are behind and reaching forward to those things which are
ahead, I press toward the goal
for the prize of the upward call
of God in Christ Jesus. Therefore let us, as many as are
mature, have this mind; and if
in anything you think other-
wise, God will reveal even this
to you. (Phil. 3:12–15)

We do not grow out of this final stage of the exchanged life— "I in Christ and Christ in me." Rather, we mature in our understanding of what it means for Christ to live His life through us. We grow in our desire to be transformed fully into His likeness and to be one with Christ. Indeed, this is the life we will experience for all eternity.

- *What new insights do you have into spiritual growth and intimacy with the heavenly Father?*

_____

_____

- *In what specific ways are you feeling challenged in your spirit today?*

_____

_____

GOD'S FORMULA FOR SPIRITUAL GROWTH (PART 1)

Most people are given advice when they are born again— it generally takes the form of things to *do* now that the person is a Christian. The advice usually includes the basics of Christian discipline: Attend church regularly, read the Bible daily, pray daily, give tithes and offerings regularly, and be faithful in service to others.

While these disciplines are vital to the Christian life, they are not a formula for spiritual growth. Rather, they are disciplines related to obeying God's commandments.

For spiritual growth, God has a much different formula. We find evidence of it in James 1:21–25, which says,

> Lay aside all filthiness and overflow of wickedness, and receive with meekness the implanted word, which is able to save your souls. But be doers of the word, and not hearers only, deceiving yourselves. For if anyone is a

hearer of the word and not a doer, he is like a man observing his natural face in a mirror; for he observes himself, goes away, and immediately forgets what kind of man he was. But he who looks into the perfect law of liberty and continues in it, and is not a forgetful hearer but a doer of the work, this one will be blessed in what he does.

- *What initial insights do you have into this passage of Scripture?*

  _____

  _____

- *How do you feel about what you read in James 1:21–25?*

  _____

  _____

If we were to reduce what James says in this passage to a "formula," it would likely be:

INSTRUCTION + INVOLVEMENT = SPIRITUAL GROWTH

We are going to take a close look at what it means to be "instructed" in this lesson, and at what it means to be "involved" in the next lesson.

Instruction

Instruction is required at every stage of spiritual growth. You needed to be "instructed" about Jesus Christ—His life and His atoning, sacrificial death—when you were in a state of unbelief. You needed to be instructed about your need for forgiveness and about God's plan for salvation. At each stage of your spiritual growth, you needed God's information about what you were experiencing, why you were experiencing it, and what a godly response should be to your experience. Instruction is absolutely vital for moving from one stage of spiritual growth to the next.

Throughout the Gospels we find Jesus instructing His disciples and others. Jesus instructed Nicodemus about his need to be born again and about what it means to believe in God's Son (see John 3:1–21). Jesus instructed a woman who came to the well at Sychar about what it means to drink of living water and about how to worship God (see John 4:5–26). Jesus taught in parables, which are "instructional stories," or stories that have a lesson of faith imbedded in them. Jesus engaged in numerous instructional sessions with His disciples, explaining to them the meaning of His parables and answering their questions. Jesus' disciples called Him "Rabbi" or "Rabboni," which means "Teacher."

Certainly one of the greatest and longest pieces of instruction in all the Bible is a passage of Scripture we call the Sermon on the Mount (see Matt. 5–7).

The epistles of Paul, Peter, and John are words of instruction, both to individuals in ministry and to the church as a whole. In Ephesians 4:11 we read that one of the main offices in the church is to be that of pastor-teacher.

God has given us His Word to instruct us. The questions we must ask ourselves are these: Am I willing to learn? Am I eager to be taught?

> • *How do you feel about your need to be "instructed" today? Are you a willing learner?*

_____

_____

Two Types of Hearers

Hearing is a significant part of instruction—not merely hearing with the ears, but hearing with "spiritual" ears, which means actively hearing with the spirit and the heart the meaning and the truth of what is being said.

Jesus said repeatedly, "He who has ears to hear, let him hear!" (Matt. 11:15; 13:9; 13:43; Mark 4:9; 4:23; 7:16; Luke 8:8; 14:35).

James identified two distinct types of hearers: careless and careful.

The Careless Hearer

The careless hearer is a hearer who is

• *deceived*. Many people falsely believe that if they hear, they understand. Hearing is not the same as knowing or understanding. It is not the same as growing, having, or experiencing. Hearing by itself is not an automatic reception of a message, neither is hearing automatically productive. We must pay close attention to what we hear and then do something with what we hear to gain genuine understanding.

• *distracted*. The distracted hearer is a person who hears, seems to comprehend, but then immediately forgets what he hears because he becomes distracted by other concerns or by new information. Many Christians are like that when it comes to last Sunday's sermon! They will tell you that it was a good sermon and they felt blessed by it, but they can't recall a thing that was actually said! Hearing requires that we focus our attention and engage our memory. We must choose to remember what we hear so that we can apply it.

• *idle*. James also states that there are those who hear and comprehend, but they never apply what they hear. To be a genuine *hearer* of the Word, we must become *doers* of the Word. We must seek to apply what we hear.

Jesus cited some of the things that cause a person to be a careless hearer. In explaining His parable of the sower to His disciples, Jesus said,

> When anyone hears the word of the kingdom, and does not understand it, then the wicked one comes and snatches away what was sown in his heart. This is he who

received seed by the wayside. But he who received the seed on stony places, this is he who hears the word and immediately receives it with joy; yet he has no root in himself, but endures only for a while. For when tribulation or persecution arises because of the word, immediately he stumbles. Now he who received seed among the thorns is he who hears the word, and the cares of this world and the deceitfulness of riches choke the word, and he becomes unfruitful. But he who received seed on the good ground is he who hears the word and understands it, who indeed bears fruit and produces: some a hundredfold, some sixty, some thirty. (Matt. 13:19–23)

• *What insights do you have about this passage of Scripture?*

_____

_____

The Careful Hearer

The careful hearer is one who

• *is intentional.* The careful hearer, James says, is one who concentrates or focuses on what he hears. He is intentional about hearing—he wants to hear and he wants to be able to act on what he hears. He actively engages his memory to remember what he hears.

• *abides by what is heard.* The careful hearer is one who attaches importance to what he hears from God's Word and seeks immediately to apply it to his life. He knows he has heard truth and he eagerly seeks ways in which to express truth. He not only wants to know what is right but to do what is right in God's eyes.

• *In your experience, can you cite times in which you have been a careless hearer? Can you recall specific times when you have been a careful hearer? What were the results in each case?*

_____

_____

What the Word Says

What the Word Says to Me

[Jesus said,] "I speak to them in parables, because seeing they do not see, and hearing they do not hear, nor do they understand. And in them the prophecy of Isaiah is fulfilled, which says:
'Hearing you will hear and shall not understand,
And seeing you will see and not perceive;
For the hearts of this people have grown dull.
Their ears are hard of hearing,
And their eyes they have closed,
Lest they should see with their eyes and hear with their ears,
Lest they should understand with their hearts and turn,
So that I should heal them.'
But blessed are your eyes for they see, and your ears for they hear." (Matt. 13:13–16)

[Jesus said,] "If anyone loves Me, he will keep My word; and My Father will love him, and We will come to him and make Our home with him. He who does not love Me does not keep My words; and the word which you hear is not Mine

but the Father's who sent Me."
(John 14:23–24)

[Jesus said,] "If you know
these things, blessed are you if
you do them." (John 13:17)

Recalling the Truth to Your Mind

Another key aspect of instruction is memory. To be truly instructed, we must not only perceive, comprehend, understand, and apply what we hear, but we must choose to remember what we have learned. We must actively choose to recall what we have been taught.

Time and again through the Scriptures, the Israelites were brought to a place of reminding themselves of God's deeds and the truth of God's word to them. The recalling of the truth to their minds nearly always led to a renewed trust in the Lord or to more active repentance. The same is true for us—the more we recall God's work in our lives and bring back to remembrance God's words to our hearts, the stronger we grow in our faith and the more eager we are to respond to God's directives. We must never forget the goodness of God or His promises to us.

There are two things we can do to keep what we have learned active and alive in our minds.

1. Memorize God's Word

Commit God's Word to memory. One of the easiest ways to memorize God's Word is to write a verse on a 3"x5" card and carry that card with you, reading the verse aloud to yourself several dozen times over the course of a few days. Not only will you be reading the verse with your eyes but you will be hearing it with your ears, which creates a double impact on your memory. After reading the verse several times, try reciting it from memory. Check your accuracy. Read the verse again a couple of times. This is a great way to make good use of your drive time, or the time you spend waiting in airports, for appointments, or for family members to get ready for events or activities.

The Lord has said that the Holy Spirit will recall to our minds the words of Jesus when we need them the most for guidance, courage, or witnessing (see John 15:26–27; 16:1–3). In order for the Lord to recall something to our minds, we first must have planted it into our minds. Routinely reading and memorizing God's Word is of great benefit to every believer, no matter how mature that believer may be.

- *What experiences have you had with memorizing God's Word?*

_____

_____

What the Word Says

If you receive my words,
And treasure my commands
within you,
So that you incline your ear to
wisdom,
And apply your heart to
understanding;
Yes, if you cry out for discernment,
And lift up your voice for
understanding,
If you seek her [wisdom] as silver,
And search for her as for hidden treasures;
Then you will understand the
fear of the LORD,

What the Word Says to Me

_____

_____

_____

_____

_____

_____

_____

_____

_____

_____

_____

_____

And find the knowledge of God.
For the LORD gives wisdom;
From His mouth come knowl-
edge and understanding;
He stores up sound wisdom
for the upright;
He is a shield to those who
walk uprightly;
He guards the paths of justice,
And preserves the way of His
saints.
Then you will understand
righteousness and justice,
Equity and every good path.
(Prov. 2:1–9)

This I recall to my mind,
Therefore I have hope. (Lam.
3:21)

[Jesus said,] "Remember the
word that I said to you, 'A servant is not greater than his
master.'" (John 15:20)

[Paul said,] "I have shown you
in every way, by laboring like
this, that you must support the
weak. And remember the
words of the Lord Jesus, that
He said, 'It is more blessed to
give than to receive.'" (Acts
20:35)

Remember the words which
were spoken before by the

apostles of our Lord Jesus
Christ: how they told you that
there would be mockers in the
last time who would walk
according to their own ungodly
lusts. (Jude 17–18)

This is the covenant that I will
make with them after those
days, says the LORD: I will put
My laws into their hearts, and
in their minds I will write
them. (Heb. 10:16)

2. Include God's Word in Your Praise and Prayers

Praise and thank God daily for what He has done for you—
and do so in the context of reciting Scripture back to the Lord.
For example, you might say, "Thank You, Lord, for providing
what I needed yesterday. Your Word that 'all things shall be
added unto you' has been proved once again!"

Pray the Scriptures. For example, you might pray, "Lord, I
am so grateful for Your Word that says, 'I am the vine and you
are the branches . . . without Me you can do nothing.' I believe
that with all my heart, Lord, and I am trusting You today to
reveal to me what I should say and do. I praise You that as I
follow the leading of Your Spirit, I will do and say those things
that are of eternal benefit."

The more you relate your life to the Scriptures and the
Scriptures to your life, the more your mind will be filled with
the truth of God's Word and the more readily the Holy Spirit
can use the Word to instruct you on a daily basis.

What the Word Says

What the Word Says to Me

Oh, give thanks to the LORD!

Call upon His name;
Make known His deeds among
the peoples!
Sing to Him, sing psalms to
Him;
Talk of all His wondrous
works!
Glory in His holy name;
Let the hearts of those rejoice
who seek the LORD!
Seek the LORD and His
strength;
Seek His face evermore!
Remember His marvelous
works which He has done,
His wonders, and the judg-
ments of His mouth. (Ps.
105:1–5)

(Read Psalm 106 as an example of an expression of praise
recounting the deeds and Word
of the Lord.)

Psalm 119 has often been called the "teaching and learning" psalm. It is a psalm that gives very specific instructions about how to receive spiritual truth into your life. I encourage you to read it fully and carefully. Note especially:

- The Lord gives His blessing to those who know and *keep* His commandments (v. 2).
- We are called to "meditate" on the Lord's precepts and to "contemplate" the Lord's ways (v. 15).
- As we "run the course" of God's commandments, the Lord enlarges our hearts (v. 32).

- Instruction produces "good judgment" as well as knowledge (v. 66).
- Meditating on God's Word makes a person wiser than his enemies (v. 98).
- We are called not only to know God's Word but to speak it (v. 172).

- *What additional insights do you have into Psalm 119?*

_____

_____

- *What new insights do you have into spiritual growth and the need for receiving instruction?*

_____

_____

- *In what ways are you feeling challenged in your spirit today?*

_____

_____

LESSON 9

GOD'S FORMULA FOR SPIRITUAL GROWTH (PART 2)

We are all called to be doers of what we learn from God's Word (see James 1:22). But how is it that we become doers? What is required for us to be adequate "doers"?

James gives us God's formula for spiritual growth:

INSTRUCTION + INVOLVEMENT = SPIRITUAL GROWTH

Doers are "those who become involved with other people in the doing of God's work." We are never called to "do God's work" in isolation. We are always called to do God's work in association with others who are of like mind and heart.

Throughout the New Testament, we have numerous references to Christians being the "body" of Christ. Our relationship with others is described as that of a family. The work of the Lord is done in a community context, each believer contributing his unique talents and spiritual gifts to the body as a whole. In this way, the gospel is spread, the needs of God's people are met, and we individually experience greater joy, love, and purpose. The process is one that results in mutual edification.

To be part of a body or a family requires one thing from us: involvement.

Involvement

Instruction, the first half of the formula for spiritual growth, may be highly personal and individualized. We learn at different rates, each of us finding unique and personal ways in which to apply what we learn. But involvement requires that we develop relationships with other people. It is in the context of relationships that we *do* what we learn from God's Word. Our doing may involve tasks, but far more important, our doing involves people.

- *How do you feel about becoming involved with other Christians in the doing of God's Word?*

_____

_____

There are many Christians who take the approach "I'm an idea person" or, "I'm task-oriented"—and they then conclude, "I'm just not a people person." The truth of God's Word is that we are all called to become "people persons." We are to be involved with other people.

Let me remind you of several familiar passages of Scripture. Note that each of these is stated in "we," "our," or other "group" terms. (Italics have been added for emphasis.)

> *Our* Father in heaven,
> Hallowed be Your name.
> Your kingdom come.

Your will be done
On earth as it is in heaven.
Give *us* this day our daily bread.
And forgive us *our* debts,
As we forgive *our* debtors. (Matt. 6:9–12)

You are the light of the world. A *city* that is set on a hill cannot be hidden. (Matt. 5:14)

The harvest truly is plentiful, but the *laborers* are few. (Matt. 9:37)

Assuredly, I say to you, unless you are converted and become as little *children*, you will by no means enter the kingdom of heaven. (Matt. 18:3)

When Jesus sent out His disciples to preach the good news, heal the sick, and deliver those who were possessed by demons, He sent them out two by two (see Mark 6:7).

- *What new insights do you have into these passages of Scripture regarding the involvement we are to have with one another?*

_____

_____

The hallmark challenge of Jesus about service was this: "Whoever desires to be first among you, let him be your slave—just as the Son of Man did not come to be served, but to serve, and to give His life a ransom for many" (Matt. 20:27–28). As Jesus served others and poured out His life for "many," we are to serve and pour out our life energy, resources, time, and talents to meet the needs of others.

A Threefold Involvement

The involvement we are to have with others is threefold:

1. *The Great Commandment: Love others.* Our supreme involvement with others is rooted in love. Jesus said,

> "You shall love the LORD your God with all your heart, with all your soul, and with all your mind." This is the first and great commandment. And the second is like it: "You shall love your neighbor as yourself." On these two commandments hang all the Law and the Prophets. (Matt. 22:37–40)

How is love expressed? By giving. We give our time, our resources, our creativity, our talents, our encouraging words, our comforting presence, our listening ears, our watchful eyes, our gifts, our prayers. And we give with the intent of blessing, of meeting needs, and of building up those to whom we give.

We give as the Lord commands us to give—generously, freely, sacrificially, and with a cheerful heart.

We are literally called to "spend ourselves" in service to others.

- *How do you feel about the Lord's command that we love our neighbors as ourselves?*

_____

_____

What the Word Says

So let each one give as he purposes in his heart, not grudgingly or of necessity; for God loves a cheerful giver. (2 Cor. 9:7)

If we love one another, God abides in us, and His love has been perfected in us. (1 John 4:12)

What the Word Says to Me

_____

_____

_____

_____

_____

_____

_____

_____

_____

He who loves God must love his brother also. (1 John 4:21)

Let us love one another, for love is of God; and everyone who loves is born of God and knows God. He who does not love does not know God, for God is love. (1 John 4:7–8)

[Jesus said,] "This is My commandment, that you love one another as I have loved you. Greater love has no one than this, than to lay down one's life for his friends." (John 15:12–13)

2. *The Great Commission: Witness to others.* Our involvement is not to be limited to those who are in the body of Christ, but rather, it is to include involvement with those who do not know the Lord so that we might lead sinners to believe in Jesus as their Savior and receive God's forgiveness of sin.

Jesus said to His disciples then and now, "Go therefore and make disciples of all the nations, baptizing them in the name of the Father and of the Son and of the Holy Spirit, teaching them to observe all things that I have commanded you; and lo, I am with you always, even to the end of the age" (Matt. 28:19–20).

To be an effective witness for Christ, we must let people know that we care about them and that we desire for them to be with us in heaven one day. We must love them as Christ loved them. Jesus gave very clear instructions about how we are to love even those who persecute us: Give to them, pray for them, and speak well of them (see Matt. 5:43–44). In this, we establish an untarnished reputation of love and kindness, and our words about Christ have a far greater appeal.

• *How do you feel about Christ's great commission that we are to take the gospel to all nations?*

_____

_____

What the Word Says

In this the love of God was manifested toward us, that God has sent His only begotten Son into the world, that we might live through Him . . . We love Him because He first loved us. (1 John 4:9, 19)

[Jesus said,] "You have heard that it was said, 'You shall love your neighbor and hate your enemy.' But I say to you, love your enemies, bless those who curse you, do good to those who hate you, and pray for those who spitefully use you and persecute you, that you may be sons of your Father in heaven . . . For if you love those who love you, what reward have you? Do not even the tax collectors do the same? And if you greet your brethren only, what do you do more

What the Word Says to Me

_____

_____

_____

_____

_____

_____

_____

_____

_____

_____

_____

_____

_____

_____

_____

_____

_____

_____

_____

_____

_____

than others?" (Matt. 5:43–45, 46–47)

[Jesus said,] "Go home to your friends, and tell them what great things the Lord has done for you, and how He has had compassion on you." (Mark 5:19)

----

3. *The Great Commitment: Serving others.* Jesus is our role model for service. On the night He was betrayed, Jesus washed the feet of His disciples—doing the job of the lowliest household servant—and He said to them about what He had done,

> Do you know what I have done to you? You call Me Teacher and Lord, and you say well, for so I am. If I then, your Lord and Teacher, have washed your feet, you also ought to wash one another's feet. For I have given you an example, that you should do as I have done to you. Most assuredly, I say to you, a servant is not greater than his master; nor is he who is sent greater than he who sent him. (John 13:12–16)

We are never to think ourselves too great, too important, too clean, too righteous, too intelligent, too wealthy, or too spiritual to undertake a task that will be a blessing to a person the Lord puts in our path. We are to give to all who ask of us—and to do so generously.

- *How do you feel about the Lord's challenge that we serve others as He served His disciples?*

What the Word Says	What the Word Says to Me
[Jesus said,] "Give to everyone who asks of you. And from him who takes away your goods do not ask them back. And just as you want men to do to you, you also do to them likewise." (Luke 6:30–31)	....
[Jesus said,] "Whoever compels you to go one mile, go with him two. Give to him who asks you, and from him who wants to borrow from you do not turn away." (Matt. 5:41–42)	....
[Jesus said,] "When you do a charitable deed, do not let your left hand know what your right hand is doing, that your charitable deed may be in secret; and your Father who sees in secret will Himself reward you openly." (Matt. 6:3–4)	....

How the Formula Works

The formula James gives for spiritual growth (INSTRUCTION + INVOLVEMENT = SPIRITUAL GROWTH) works in this way:

The more we hear God's Word as careful hearers—diligent in our search for God's meaning and truth, and eager to remember God's Word and apply it to our daily lives—the more we will actually seek to apply or do God's Word.

The more we apply God's Word to our lives—putting it to the test and "trying it out"—the more we discover that God's Word *works*. Others around us are impacted in two ways. They are the recipients of our godly behavior, including our godly speech. Those who are impacted for good by what we do and say are likely to ask us (or another godly person) what motivates us to do good. This gives us an opportunity to witness about the love and forgiveness and personal presence of the Lord in our lives. We grow spiritually as we share our faith.

Or, those around us may be influenced by our behavior to engage in godly behavior, adopt godly attitudes, or display godly speech themselves. As they put God's truth into practical effect in their own lives, they will also discover that it works and they will want to continue to do good.

The more that we see God's truth as practical and producing a blessing in our lives, the more eager we will be to learn even more about God's ways, plans, and purposes. And the more we learn, the more we will want to apply God's truth. The cycle continues and builds, and what we do and say influences others in an ever-widening circle of influence and witness. As part of this process, we *grow* spiritually and we find ourselves drawing closer and closer to the heart of God.

- *In your experience as a Christian, recall and reflect upon an experience in which instruction and involvement with others produced spiritual growth in your life.*

_____

_____

The Lord promises a great blessing to those who seek to grow spiritually. Not only does He promise us His infinite and awesome presence, but He promises to meet our deepest needs. The more our needs are met, the greater our appreciation and love for God grow. And the greater our love for God grows, the more we delight in spending time with Him. God is no longer a far-off stranger to us, but rather, our nearest and dearest Friend and the One on whom we rely for unconditional love, acceptance, and fellowship.

- *How do you feel about God being your best Friend, the One who knows you and loves you as no other ever can?*

_____

_____

What the Word Says

[Jesus said,] "No longer do I call you servants, for a servant does not know what his master is doing; but I have called you friends, for all things that I heard from My Father I have made known to you." (John 15:15)

Because he has set his love upon Me, therefore I will deliver him;
I will set him on high, because he has known My name.
He shall call upon Me, and I will answer him;
I will be with him in trouble;
I will deliver him and honor him.
With long life I will satisfy him,
And show him My salvation.
(Ps. 91:14–16)

What the Word Says to Me

_____

_____

_____

_____

_____

_____

_____

_____

_____

_____

_____

_____

_____

_____

_____

_____

_____

_____

_____

- *What new insights do you have into spiritual growth?*

  _____

  _____

- *In what ways are you feeling challenged in your spirit?*

  _____

  _____

LESSON 10

TIME APART WITH THE LORD

There is one final key to spiritual growth that is perhaps the greatest secret of all. It certainly is a factor in every stage of spiritual growth. It is perhaps the foremost factor that gives rise to all requirements for spiritual growth. The key is this: spending time alone with the Lord.

King David has been called a "man after God's own heart." To be a man *after* God's own heart means that David needed first to know the mind and heart of God so that he might be and do what the Lord desired of him. David sought to know God. He frequently "inquired" of the Lord. He spent time in the Lord's presence singing to the Lord from the depths of his heart. In 2 Samuel 7:18 we read,

> Then King David went in and sat before the LORD; and said: "Who am I, O Lord GOD? And what is my house, that You have brought me this far?"

What does it mean for David to "sit" before the Lord? It means that he spent time alone in the presence of the Lord, communicating with the Lord from the depths of his heart, asking questions of God, and listening quietly before the Lord for the Lord's answers.

- *Have you had experiences in spending time alone with the Lord?*

_____

_____

- *How do you feel about the idea of spending time with the Lord?*

_____

_____

Jesus frequently sought time apart with His heavenly Father. Time with the Father was a source of comfort and strength to Him. Jesus also sought time alone with His disciples so that He might teach them and they might be refreshed spiritually (see Luke 9:10).

When we choose to spend time with the Lord, we are wise to spend this time alone with Him, in a place where we will not be distracted or interrupted, for a period of time sufficient for us to relax completely and focus our attention fully upon the Lord and His Word. We must be willing to wait in the Lord's presence until we receive God's directives or His words of comfort and edification.

- *In your experience, where is the best time for you to spend time with the Lord?*

_____

_____

Why People Don't Spend Time with God

There are a number of reasons people don't desire to spend time alone with God. The foremost reason is that they aren't sure of their relationship with God and therefore, they are afraid of God.

Those who are born again spiritually have a Father-child relationship with the Lord. Our heavenly Father loves us unconditionally and is tender and patient in His dealings with us. If we do not perceive God in this manner, however, we tend to avoid God and are fearful of spending time alone in His presence. If you are reluctant to spend time apart with the Lord, consider these questions:

- Do you perceive God as loving, or demanding?
- Do you perceive God as near, or distant?
- Do you perceive God as being patient, or intolerant?
- Do you perceive God as gentle, or angry?
- Do you perceive God as understanding, or insensitive?
- Do you perceive God as generous, or stingy?
- Do you perceive God as faithful, or inconsistent?

What you believe about God will determine greatly the amount of time you spend with God, and the attitude you have toward God when you are in His presence.

- *How do your own feelings about God impact your desire to spend time with God?*

_____

_____

The Blessings of Time Alone with God

The Bible speaks of many great blessings that come from spending time alone with the Lord. As you read the passage below from the Psalms, note the very specific rewards of meditation—which for the Christian may be defined as quiet contemplation about God's Word in God's presence:

Oh, how I love Your law!
It is my meditation all the day.

You, through Your commandments, make me wiser than
my enemies;
For they are ever with me.
I have more understanding than all my teachers,
For Your testimonies are my meditation.
I understand more than the ancients,
Because I keep Your precepts.
I have restrained my feet from every evil way,
That I may keep Your word.
I have not departed from Your judgments,
For You Yourself have taught me.
How sweet are Your words to my taste,
Sweeter than honey to my mouth!
Through Your precepts I get understanding;
Therefore I hate every false way. (Ps. 119:97–104)

Those who spend time alone with the Lord find comfort,
hope, and joy in His presence. They find themselves being built
up, from the inside out, and they generally emerge from a time
with the Lord feeling refreshed and more courageous as they
face their needs or tackle their problems.

- *What has been your experience in spending time with the
  Lord? What have been the results in your life?*

_____

_____

What the Word Says

He who dwells in the secret
place of the Most High
Shall abide under the shadow
of the Almighty.
I will say of the LORD, "He is
my refuge and my fortress;
My God, in Him I will trust."
(Ps. 91:1–2)

What the Word Says to Me

_____

_____

_____

_____

_____

_____

_____

[Jesus said,] "Come to Me, all you who labor and are heavy laden, and I will give you rest . . . Learn from Me, for I am gentle and lowly in heart, and you will find rest for your souls." (Matt. 11:28–29)

What Do We Do?

There are four helpful things that you can *do* as you spend time apart with the Lord. These are things that can lead to your hearing the voice of God in fresh, invigorating ways:

1. Review the Past

As David sat in the presence of the Lord, he no doubt remembered his fight with Goliath, his years of successfully avoiding Saul's murderous intent, and the battles he had won. In the passage that we noted above, David had just heard from the prophet Nathan that the Lord was going to establish his house, his kingdom, and his throne forever (see 2 Sam. 7:16–17). David no doubt reviewed God's many blessings to him in the past as he weighed these wonderful words from Nathan.

As you sit in the Lord's presence, reflect on all that the Lord has done for you, in you, and through you. David wrote,

> Enter into His gates with thanksgiving,
> And into His courts with praise.
> Be thankful to Him, and bless His name.
> For the LORD is good;
> His mercy is everlasting,
> And His truth endures to all generations. (Ps. 100:4–5)

- *What new insights do you have into this passage of Scripture?*

---

2. Reflect upon God

Spend time reflecting upon the awesome nature of God. Especially focus on His greatness, His grace to you, and His goodness. Spend time contemplating the many names of God and Jesus in the Scriptures—each name reflects a facet of the Lord's nature. Consider these attributes of God:

Eternal	Loving
Faithful	Merciful
Good	All-Powerful (Omnipotent)
Gracious	All-Wise (Omniscient)
Holy	Ever-Present
Immutable	(Omnipresent)
Jealous	Righteous
Just	Sovereign
Long-suffering	

The more we put our attention on our great, awesome, and loving God—who sent His only begotten Son to die for our sins so that we might be reconciled to Him and live with Him forever in heaven—the smaller our problems seem.

What the Word Says	What the Word Says to Me
Oh, how great is Your goodness, Which You have laid up for those who fear You, Which You have prepared for those who trust in You In the presence of the sons of men! (Ps. 31:19)	----------------------------------- ----------------------------------- ----------------------------------- ----------------------------------- ----------------------------------- ----------------------------------- -----------------------------------
The LORD is my strength and my shield; My heart trusted in Him, and	----------------------------------- ----------------------------------- -----------------------------------

I am helped;
Therefore my heart greatly
rejoices,
And with my song I will praise
Him. (Ps. 28:7)

Through the LORD's mercies
we are not consumed,
Because His compassions fail
not.
They are new every morning;
Great is Your faithfulness.
"The LORD is my portion,"
says my soul,
"Therefore I hope in Him!"
The LORD is good to those
who wait for Him,
To the soul who seeks Him.
It is good that one should hope
and wait quietly
For the salvation of the LORD.
(Lam. 3:22–26)

3. Remember God's Promises

God has made numerous promises throughout His Word regarding your provision, protection, and potential to receive His blessings. As you spend time with the Lord, thank Him for His promises even as you recount them and reread them aloud. Allow God's promises to kindle your faith—for surely, what God has said, God will do. He is faithful at all times to His own Word!

What the Word Says

What the Word Says to Me

[The Lord spoke through
Isaiah,]

"I am God, and there is no
other;
I am God, and there is none
like Me,
Declaring the end from the
beginning,
And from ancient times things
that are not yet done,
Saying, 'My counsel shall
stand,
And I will do all My pleasure,' . . .
Indeed I have spoken it;
I will also bring it to pass.
I have purposed it;
I will also do it." (Isa. 46:9–11)

The Lord is faithful, who will
establish you and guard you
from the evil one. (2 Thess.
3:3)

He who calls you is faithful,
who also will do it. (1 Thess.
5:24)

4. Make Requests of the Lord Regarding Your Spiritual Growth

As you spend time alone with the Lord, after thanking Him
for His many acts of mercy and kindness in the past, reflecting upon His goodness and love, and remembering His
promises . . . ask the Lord for those things that you desire the
most:

- Ask the Lord to give you His perspective on your
  problems, needs, relationships, and opportunities.

- Ask the Lord to give you His peace.
- Ask the Lord to give you a positive attitude and to help you forgive those who may have hurt you, rejected you, or disappointed you.
- Ask the Lord to purify your thoughts.
- Ask the Lord to give you a passion to obey Him.
- Ask the Lord to direct all of your steps.

The Lord delights in answering petitions such as these.

And Then, Listen

Most important, as you spend time alone with the Lord, listen. Simply sit quietly in the Lord's presence and allow Him to speak to you. So often we come into the Lord's presence and we do nothing but talk. Although our praises, thanksgiving, and reading of Scripture are right things to speak to the Lord, it is also right that we wait quietly in His presence. Psalm 46:10 wisely admonishes us, "Be still, and know that I am God."

The Lord delights in speaking to the willing heart. He delights in "growing us up" into the likeness of His Son. He delights in revealing to us His plan and purpose for our lives. He delights in encouraging us with His presence, empowering us to do His will, and embracing us tenderly when we need His comfort.

Choose to spend time alone with the Lord. Truly there is no more important way to spend your time!

- *What new insights do you have into spiritual growth and intimacy with God?*

  _____

  _____

- *In what ways are you feeling challenged in your spirit?*

  _____

  _____

THE LORD DESIRES YOUR PRESENCE

We said at the outset of this book that the Lord has issued a wonderful invitation to each of us to come into His presence and to grow into His likeness. The Lord's desire is that you might know Him, love Him, serve Him, and live with Him forever. The Lord's desire is to have an intimate, personal relationship with you.

As is appropriate with many invitations, a response is requested from you. What will your response be today? Will you accept God's invitation? Will you choose to grow in your relationship with Him until you experience genuine intimacy with Christ, your Creator and Savior and Lord?